# That Is What We Are
Max Austin

Copyright © by Max Austin.

Artwork: Adobe Stock – © pixelrobot, Sweta, Papapig.

Cover designed by Spectrum Books.

All rights reserved.

Paperback ISBN: 978-1-915905-24-6

No part of this book may be used or reproduced in any manner whatsoever without written permission of the author of Spectrum Books, except for brief quotations used for promotion or in reviews. This book is a work of fiction. Names, characters, places and events are fictitious.

First edition, Spectrum Books, 2024

Discover more LGBTQ+ books at www.spectrum-books.com

# Contents

| | |
|---|---|
| Chapter One | 3 |
| Chapter Two | 10 |
| Chapter Three | 19 |
| Chapter Four | 28 |
| Chapter Five | 35 |
| Chapter Six | 49 |
| Chapter Seven | 55 |
| Chapter Eight | 67 |
| Chapter Nine | 79 |
| Chapter Ten | 93 |
| Chapter Eleven | 102 |
| Chapter Twelve | 111 |
| Chapter Thirteen | 129 |
| Chapter Fourteen | 142 |
| Chapter Fifteen | 154 |
| Chapter Sixteen | 162 |
| Chapter Seventeen | 170 |
| Chapter Eighteen | 179 |

| | |
|---|---|
| Chapter Nineteen | 189 |
| Chapter Twenty | 197 |
| Chapter Twenty-One | 209 |
| Chapter Twenty-Two | 218 |
| Chapter Twenty-Three | 226 |
| Chapter Twenty-Four | 234 |

*This is for all those who've felt voiceless.*

# Chapter One

My therapist had no idea what I was talking about, but listened anyway. His brown eyes and bushy black eyebrows seemed to be willing me on. The endless meetings, report writing and budgetary requests didn't float my boat. These evils took me further and further away from the bedside. This worked for many nurse leaders, but it wasn't for me. After four years, my ward manager uniform felt like a strait-jacket every time I put it on. It was hard enough to admit this to myself, let alone anyone else. God knows what my family would say. Pongo sighed, smacked his liquorice lips and snuggled into my chest. Dogs are great like that; they don't always understand the words but love you, anyway.

I slid on wet leaves and stumbled out of the car. Wayne caught hold of my arm before I came face to face with the autumn mush. The house looked perfectly normal on the outside. In fact, it was just like every other one on King Street. These bay-fronted red-bricked villas had bread like rabbits whilst Victoria was on her throne. A series of tarnished garden gnomes led us down a tiled path and toward an entrance porch. Oh, my God! A hidden wind chime frightened me half to death. I caught my breath and glanced at a menagerie of wooden hearts, crystals and angel wings weighing down the branches of a weeping willow. Instead of a doorbell, we rang our arrival on a corded school bell. Incense hit the back of my throat as a purple door creaked open. I half imagined 'Lurch' to appear and growl 'Yurse'. But to my relief, a woman bobbed from the smoke wearing a pair of black slacks and a matching polar-necked jumper. She had pulled her dyed-black hair into a sensible bun that rested on her plump face. A touch of rouge tried but failed to hide her wrinkles. She peered up from a pair of half-moon glasses that rested on her cheeks whilst fiddling with a large rose quartz crystal that hung over her chest. In my mind's eye, I was expecting some sort of turbaned, caftan-wearing Hollywood movie star.

"Lovely to see you, you're my three o'clock. Yes, I remember, it's Max and Wayne, isn't it?

"Y-yes, that's right, it's nice to meet you too. Are you Mrs Derby?" I said.

"Come in, my dears, you'll catch your death out there."

A Minton-tiled hallway snaked its way past a plethora of different-shaped gilded mirrors that hung on emerald damask wallpaper. I noticed a display of Buddhas sitting on a buckling hallway table. A carved bowl nestled into the middle of the shrine. Mrs Derby clocked my interest. "It's my honesty bowl, my dears. Just drop something into it on the way out. But not to worry either way."

And with that, she ushered us into her lounge. Refracted colours danced from the crystals hanging in a large bay window. On the mantlepiece, I noticed a large amethyst geode surrounded by smaller but equally stunning crystals. An ornate chandelier was trying to steal the show by casting its fragmented beauty around the tall ceilings. My feet sank into the pile of a large oriental rug that partially covered the stripped pine floorboards. I imagined a gloomy candlelit room, a velvet-covered round table, a crystal ball and a potted aspidistra. Before I knew it, Wayne and I were sitting opposite Mrs Derby on a velvet ruby sofa. She plumped her cushion on her wing-backed chair, sat forward, and said,

"Well, what were you expecting? I'm sorry my dears, but I'm saving the theatre props for Halloween. Now call me Gladys. Mrs Derby is all too formal for my liking. Are you ready to begin?"

"Yes, I think so."

Gladys breathed deeply, closed her eyes for a second, and then looked at me directly. She said,

"Please don't tell me anything about you. I already know your names, and for now, that's enough. Before we start properly, let me tell you a bit about how I work. I don't get to pick and choose, so I can't guarantee anything. There's no exact science to this. Why am I hearing Dolly Parton's music? Does that mean anything? Ah, right, it all makes sense now. I have a young man with me who's desperate to talk to you. He's coming through loud and clear."

"Yes, yes," I sobbed whilst gripping onto Wayne's hand for sheer life.

Gladys seemed to be talking to someone who was invisible. She looked up from the left of her chair. "Slow down, young man. I'm a medium and not a brain surgeon. I know you have so much to say, but just be patient. Yes, yes, Jack, I can hear and see you now. Just relax."

"Did you say, Jack?" I asked.

She looked at Wayne and me directly and laughed. "Oh my goodness, yes, your Jack's a feisty one, isn't he? He's standing directly next to me and wearing a nurse's tunic top with lilac epilates. He wore that when you met him. And why is he laughing about a bed bath?"

"We had to do this during our health care assistant training. He took the mickey out of me for years about that. I'd kill him for bringing that up if he wasn't already dead."

Gladys corrected me. "No, he certainly isn't dead. He's just living on the other side of the bar until it's your time to meet again."

Now talking to Jack, she said, "Slow down young man. Yes, I'll tell them."

"Tell us what, Jack?"

Gladys took a deep breath and sighed. "Shh, it's all right, Jack. Just take your time, my dear. I can hear you loud and clear, yes I'll tell Max.

"Jack is so sorry for not being completely honest with you. He was trying to protect you but now realises that he's hurt you. You had to find out the 'hard way' about his mother, his father, and his brother. He was standing in your kitchen watching his secrets tumble out when Carla put two and two together. He loves you and wouldn't want to hurt you. He knows that you have been angry with him."

"Oh my god Jack, it's OK, I'm sorry, I love you so much, I miss you. Why did you have to leave me?"

Gladys was listening intently to Jack. She explained, "He's telling me he knows you love him and miss him, but simply put, it was his time to move on. Oh, my dear Jack, what did you just say? Do you want me to relay that message to Max?

"He's laughing now. You're still asking him for his reassurance. Just spin that roulette wheel until it comes off its hinges. It's OK to change your mind, Max. Just do what makes you happy. Life is too short to be miserable.

"He wants to say thank you for everything you've done for him. When his coffin almost hailed the bus outside the church during his funeral, he burst out laughing. He hasn't gone anywhere Max, you just can't see him. He's so proud of you.

"What did you say, Jack? Tell me again? He wants me to tell you that in a few years, you won't recognise yourself. Wayne and you are in for the ride of your life. He'll be watching over you both, pushing you on like a fairy godmother."

"Well, that sounds like him all over," I said, "but what does he mean by 'the ride of our lives'?"

Nodding towards her left again, and then turning slowly towards us, Gladys smirked and said,

"He's telling me that is for him to know and for the pair of you to find out. It's nothing bad, though."

"Well, the bloody hell, Jack, wherever you are, you're still teasing me. Just know that I love you so much."

"He loves you all. He's now talking about someone named Danni. She doesn't believe in any of this 'mumbo-jumbo' as she calls it, but tell her she's wrong," Gladys stopped for a second as if tuning her ear into a radio station before continuing, "he wants me to make sure that Danni knows that he's had the last laugh. For some strange reason, he's talking about trying to find a TV reception. Did he live with her at one point?"

"Yes, he did, and I know exactly what he's on about. Danni will be gob-smacked when I tell her this."

"And who's Miss Nancy Eclair? Ah, yes, Adam, that makes sense now. He's telling me that Adam still blames himself. This is the reason he left. Max, please tell Adam that his death had nothing to do with him. He wants you to tell Adam to take the world by the horns and shake out every drop from it. Slow down young man, yes I'll tell them, just give me a chance. Jack's over the moon that Carla and his brother Christian have married. Carla is the right woman to keep him grounded. Jack wants you to look after them both for him."

"That goes without saying Jack, you don't need to ask me that," I said.

"Yes, he knows that, but Jack knows also that sometimes you do and say things without thinking them through properly."

"He's still calling shade from the other side, but he's right. Don't worry, I already have Carla under my wing and what's another tater in the pot?"

Gladys now turned her attention to Wayne, who was sitting quietly beside me. "Jack wants to talk to you, too. He's laughing and is telling me you deserve a medal for putting up with Max. He wants me to tell you he has met up with your twin brother, Michael. They are two peas in the same spirit pod."

Wayne looked stunned. I thought he was going to drop to the floor. Somehow, he said,

"I didn't even know my brother's name. He died in childbirth. I've always blamed myself that I lived, and he didn't."

"Oh my dear, wipe your tears. Michael is happy in spirit. Wayne, he looks just like you. He's telling me it's not your fault that he died. He says that he's with you when you need him the most. You have seen him on a few occasions, haven't you?"

"Yes, that's right, I have."

Gladys passed Wayne a tissue. "Michael loves you. He says if you focus, you can see and talk to him whenever you want. But you know that deep down, right? Oh my goodness, I could be out of a job soon. Well I never! You can see and talk to spirit too!"

"I thought I was going mad. It's not something that I advertise."

Gladys laughed. "Yes, everyone thinks they're going mad at first. That happened to me too. You must come to my development circle. You're a natural. It runs every Thursday evening at seven. Jack and Michael are telling me you can see them and are catching some of their words."

"That's right, I can. But I was too scared to tell anyone about it. You see, I couldn't speak until the age of eight. Everyone had written me off as the poor little deaf boy without speech. I didn't realise that I was playing with spirit children in my silent world. It all seemed perfectly normal to me. It wasn't until years later that I clicked I could see spirit. And then I purposely ignored it. I had enough going on this side of life to contend with. I didn't want people to admit me to a mental health hospital, so I just kept quiet."

Oh my God, Jack and Michael just outed Wayne. Ever likely he had some reservations about meeting Gladys. When I booked the appointment, I thought he was just nervous. I'd no clue about any of this.

Gladys coughed and looked at the clock. "Jack and Michael are saying that they can't hang around for much longer this evening. Jack is laughing and telling me he has a date with Saint Peter. He says that you will know what that means. And just before he goes, he wants to say that he loves you all. Goodbye, my dears."

Jack and Michael had left the building.

Gladys closed her eyes for a second and stretched. "Well, that was a beautiful reading. It was a pleasure to meet Jack and Michael. I could feel the love that they've got for you both. Wayne, you are welcome to come to my development group, but I'll let you think about it. Goodness me, is that the time?"

Standing up, we wiped our eyes and casually dropped money into the honesty bowl on our way out. There was so much to talk about. But for now, a hug was all that was needed.

# Chapter Two

It had always worked in the past, so gathering the troops at the Potters Arms seemed the logical thing to do. The familiar smell of freshly served beer floating over the frivolity soon calmed my nerves. Wayne and I huddled around a table and waited for the rest of the war cabinet to arrive. Recently, the pub had changed hands. Simon and Zuri were now firmly at the helm. Simon, a brunette prince charming, worked the bar and flirted with his customers to keep them happy as he pulled his pints. He certainly put his training as one-quarter of a male review act to good use here. The male customers wanted to be like him, and well, the female patrons just wanted him. But he only had eyes for his rippled god Zuri, who was standing behind him at the bar. Zuri would not have looked out of place as an African god of war. He was an equally popular source of eye candy with the local drinking fraternity at the Potters. Both men had grown tired of baby oil and greasy hands on their bodies night after night and had opted to return home together and set up a new life. They wore matching black chinos and a crisp white shirt with the pub's name embroidered into the breast pocket. In all honesty, they could've worn a bin bag and still looked fantastic.

The bar's fittings and fixtures weren't the only things that got a makeover. Well, no one could expect such fine figures of manhood to stand on their balls night after night in a run-down boozer. It would be like using Michelangelo's David as a coat rack in the Porter's Lodge. So out was the sticky mahogany, balding floral Axminster, the ripped green vinyl seating and the over-painted woodchip that had served us well for many years. Only when I saw the complete transformation did I realise how desperate the boozer was to be taken kicking and screaming into the nineties. And what a transformation it was. They replaced the low-budget nineteen-seventies porn movie set with New England chic. The white-washed bar, navy and white cushioned chairs, stripped pine tables and chalky walls were just the right side of nautical to be tasteful. Instead of giving us the feeling of standing on the deck of the Titanic before it sank, it transported us to a Lakeside retreat. Even the food offering had been upgraded. Where once cardboard racks of peanuts or pork scratchings had hung, there was now a smart chalkboard offering an American twist on local delicacies. So instead of an obligatory traditional soggy bacon and cheese oatcake, people were now offered 'a crisp grilled oatcake with streaky bacon and Colby -Jack filling'. Even some of the beer taps had been changed in favour of trying bespoke guest ales. These changes were as thoroughly welcome, delicious and tantalising as Simon and Zuri themselves.

Danni was the first to sail in. She plonked herself and those bloody awful parrot earrings down beside us. As much as I tried to get her to move with the times, she still insisted on wearing them. Luckily, the rest of her was not stuck in the eighties. There was certainly a spring in her step these days for some reason only known to her. If there was one thing that I had learnt over the years, it was best to leave sleeping dogs lying until our queen of mystery was ready to reveal her secrets. Apart from her offending wildlife, she looked more like Marie Fredricsson every time I saw her. Danni looked stunning in a pair of tight leather trousers, a Rolling Stones T-shirt, and a figure-hugging black denim jacket. It was just a pity that she couldn't sing because she could have made a fortune belting out 'It Must Have Been Love' to the backdrop of our very own Chippendales behind the bar.

Christian and Carla swiftly followed Danni. Every time I saw Christian, I had to take a second glance. He looked so much like his brother, and this alone comforted me. I'm sure that he even wore the same aftershave as my fallen tin soldier, too. Carla instinctively understood my fondness for him and smiled at him every time she noticed me breathing him in. The newlyweds looked so beautifully tanned after a couple of weeks on their Majorcan honeymoon. Christian wore a pair of blue jeans and a white linen shirt. Carla looked stunning in a pale blue flounce-sleeve lace dress with her brown locks loosely tied into a ponytail. She was positively glowing from head to foot. Aunt Bren was the last to arrive. I knew it was pathetic, but I figured I could hide behind her purple skirt if the conversation got bumpy later in the evening. It was tight, but we all just about squeezed around the wonky table top together.

It wasn't long before Aunt Bren had us in stitches as she tried to flirt with our hosts. She slowly rose to her feet and insisted on getting the first round of drinks. As she jangled over the bar, I just about grabbed her before she toppled over. Undressing Simon and Zuri from behind the twinkle of her mascaraed eyes, she said,

"Well, you don't get many of you in a pound, do you? Come here and let me hug you. Don't worry, you're quite safe. I've had my fill of stud muffins. Did you know that my late husband and I ran this pub together? If only these walls could talk. You've done a lovely job with the old place though. Now, if you need any tips, then just ask me?"

"Yes, as a matter of fact, we knew you ran the pub for many years. Max told us," Zuri replied.

"I bet he did too. A girl can't have any secrets when he's around. If I didn't love him so much, I'd wash his mouth out with soap and water. Anyway, it's a pleasure to meet you both. I wish you nothing but love and happiness in your new home together. Now serve me the bloody beer. My throat is as dry as the bottom of a budgie's cage."

It wasn't long before we were all suitably lubricated. Carla was content with a bottle of cola. She must have been driving. Danni smirked, wiped her hands on her thighs and said,

"Well Carla, let's have it, how was the honeymoon?"

"It was perfect, thank you. We had a beautiful time didn't we Christian?"

"Yes, we did. I'm the luckiest man alive. We've got an announcement to make. My beautiful wife over there is expecting. We've been bursting to tell you."

The table broke down into tears of joy. It was the best thing that we had all heard in ages. Pulling myself back from cloud nine, I winked, put the back of my hand over my forehead and said, "Well, I suppose you will want maternity leave now. Look at you, only my deputy for five minutes and already wanting more time off.

"I'm not being unreasonable here, but can you just have the baby and come back to work on the next shift? You've had two weeks off for your wedding already and now you'll want maternity leave. It's just not fair, Carla. I'm running a ward and not the Marie Celeste. How could you do this to me?"

"Trust you, Max. I'm so sorry to put you out and all."

"Well, you can have the time off on one condition only. You must solemnly promise me that as soon as the baby pops its head into the world, you call it Max. You see, it works for either a boy or a girl, so there is no excuse, is there?"

"Sorry, Max, I can't promise you that."

"Come here and give me a massive hug. I am so chuffed for you both."

The table swayed and the drinks flowed. Only Carla remained in control of her faculties. I caught hold of Wayne's hand under the table. I knew that this conversation would not be easy by any stretch of the imagination, but I felt duty-bound to make sure that Jack's voice was heard in our group. By the time I had finished relaying the story of our recent trip to see Gladys Derby, they were stunned into silence. As predicted, Danni was the first to show her cards. I recognised her sharp features far too well and got ready to go into battle with her. Before I had the chance to make my move, she jumped in and said,

Why on earth did you visit that old witch doctor Max? And to make matters worse, why did you drag Wayne into all of this?"

"Gladys Derby is well known at the hospital for being nothing more than a fraud. It's no mistake that she has set up her freak show so close to the City Infirmary. This is the ideal location for her to trap the vulnerable and bereaved in her web of lies.

"I thought you would've had more brains than to get yourself mixed up in all of this mumbo jumbo. For all you know, she could have already known about Jack's death. This type of evil vulture scours the local 'births and deaths' column' of the paper for information. It really wouldn't take her long to put two and two together, now would it?"

Before I had the chance to reply, I felt a strong waft of Avon perfume under my nostrils as Aunt Bren stood to my defence. She scowled at Danni. "Just tell me who the bloody hell you think you are, lady? People in glass houses shouldn't throw stones, should they Danni? Although I am grateful for all you've done for Max, you've no right to speak to him or anyone like this. Wind your pigging neck and put a sock in it!"

You could cut the atmosphere in the pub with a knife. The gentle banter that normally circulated over the boozer fell into silence. The regulars watched the commotion coming from our table. There's nothing like getting your dirty washing out in public to create such entertainment.

It was now my turn to speak. "Danni, I love you, I do, but I'm afraid you're wrong about this. How would Gladys know about the incident with the TV Ariel reception? No one outside of our circle knows about that, thank god. There was just too much detail for her to be making it up. She even said that you would struggle to accept this information. But it was Jack, Danni. He was there in spirit."

Danni was cornered and shaking. I had no idea what she would do next as she rubbed her hand up and down her leathers. And then she broke her silence. "I'm so sorry. I can be such a hard cow, can't I? Bren's right to put me in my place."

I guess this wasn't the best time for Wayne to reveal his news about Michael, though. This would have properly finished Danni off. She may have apologised, but she was still frothing over like a pint of stale beer.

Who in the name of Satan on a scooter was ringing our doorbell at this hour? And if it was the god squad, then they could just bog off. It may have been ten-thirty in the morning, but after all the kerfuffle of the previous evening, it took Wayne and me until the small hours to feel tired enough to sleep. Pongo welcomed our unwelcome visitor over the doorstep whilst my eyes adjusted to the daylight. With my dressing gown cord firmly tied around my waist, I rolled my shoulders and got ready for round two. She silently followed me into the kitchen, plonked herself down at the table and drummed her nails on a plastic placemat while waiting for the kettle to boil. Every tap felt like a drill going off in my head, but instead of rising to the bait, I busied myself preparing the morning brew. The smell of warm dog's breath filled the room. I wasn't sure if it was mine or Pongo's and to be honest; I didn't care. Tea spilled from the cup as I slammed it down before her. Looking directly into her eyes, I said,

"The words 'sorry' might have been coming out of your mouth, but I am not buying any of your crap. You were as angry as all hell with me. If it wasn't for Aunt Bren, I dread to think what you would have said and done. I loved him too, Danni. You don't get the monopoly on grief."

"And that's why I'm here now. I don't want to fall out with you. I'm sorry for my behaviour last night. I don't know what came over me."

"The thing is, it's not the first time that you've flown off the handle at me, is it? You need to learn to tame those blonde spikes. We all hurt."

She smiled and nodded. "Yes, you are right. I remember the days when you thought I walked on water and now look at us both. Bitching in the kitchen together."

And with that, I laughed, leaned in and gave her a slobbery kiss on her cheek before it was too late for her to clock that it was me that stunk and not Pongo. Wayne appeared, freshly showered and smelling wonderful. He dried his brown locks with a towel as he sat down with us. I didn't bat an eyelid as my half-clad Adonis dripped into his drink before casually throwing a shirt over his broad torso and steaming up Danni's glasses. For once, I could tell what she was thinking. And she was right. I was very lucky to curl up to him every night. I still had no idea what he saw in me.

Now that her windscreen had cleared, I looked into her eyes. It was about time to mention the elephant that had been patiently waiting in the corner of the room. I swigged a mouthful of tea and piped up, "I know you mean well, Danni. You're just trying to protect me, as always. I get it, I do. But Jack was there. Gladys was genuine, she knew the personal stuff. She wasn't trying to fleece us, either."

"What do you mean by that? What's wrong with you, Max? Is something bad going on between the two of you?"

I glanced at Wayne, smiled, and said, "No worries, we're rock solid. I don't know what I would do without him. My head has been in the shed for a while and I just wanted to hear that Jack is OK. I miss him."

"Yes, we all miss him. I'm just struggling with the whole 'medium thing'. I've heard so many bad things about these so-called psychics. And I'm not convinced about life after death and all of that. You shocked me last night. I'm worried about you Max, what do you mean by 'head in the shed' exactly?"

Danni was going nowhere until I had come clean. She shuffled, leaned on an elbow, and helped herself to a custard cream whilst waiting patiently for me to speak. Somehow, Pongo had pushed his head right over my lap. I didn't realise that I had been playing with his velvet ears until he licked my hand. I took a deep breath. "Danni, I love my life, I do, but something is missing. I can't put my finger on what it is yet. There is one thing that I am completely certain about. Please don't be angry, but I don't want to do my job anymore. You know better than anyone that I didn't become a nurse to sit in an office and pen push."

Danni sighed, nodded, and then gently fist-bumped my arm. "Now, I understand. Yes, Jack's death has done odd things to us all, hasn't it? We say that we are OK, but it just takes time to find your way. I just want the best for you, that's all. It may take you a while to figure out how to fill a Jack-sized hole in your heart. But the rest, I can help with."

"Thank you. You've got a heart of gold. I feel better for telling you what is going on in this rather strange head of mine."

"No worries. By the way, did you know that the university has received funding for another cohort of trainee advanced nurse practitioners? Maybe have a chat with Eunice and Jan at work. I reckon you could have a good chance of getting on it. We're only looking for experienced nurses at ward manager level or above."

Suddenly, I could hear that roulette wheel clattering in my head again.

# Chapter Three

After getting her fingers well and truly burnt with Doctor John Stokes, lust, attraction, love, or whatever you want to call it, was the last thing on her mind. But Malcolm had other ideas. He noticed Danni several times at the 'Potters Arms' but couldn't gather the courage to start a conversation. He knew he was a seven at best and had no business shooting above his league. Anyway, what would he say to this ice maiden? She was far more preoccupied with her group of friends than to notice a short-arse lorry driver smiling at her. And he was more comfortable humming along to the likes of George Jones or Garth Brookes than chatting up beautiful women. John Denver was always his go-to. In his soundproof waggon, the mere first few bars of *Almost Heaven, West Virginia, Blue Ridge Mountains, Shenandoah River* crackling from his tinny tape deck would get him joining in. But tonight, something was different. This woman was worth the chance of public humiliation. He slammed down his empty coke glass on the freshly lacquered bar, received a smirk of encouragement from Zuri and strode over to Danni before he had the chance to change his mind again. Quizzing the barman for information beforehand was a stroke of genius. At least he knew her name, her occupation and the fact that she was single before making his move.

Danni felt a tap on her shoulder and turned around from her conversation with Wayne to see a stocky man dressed in a brown and cream lumberjack shirt, a blue denim waistcoat and a pair of ill-fitting jeans. What did he want? She had already given her donation to the Sally Army collection earlier in the evening. He wiped his sandy mullet from off his brown eyes, adjusted his silver-rimmed glasses and said,

"Is it Danni?"

Annoyed by his intrusion, she looked down her nose at the man. "Well, I guess that depends on who's asking."

"I'm asking. Apologies for the interruption. I just wanted to chat, that's all."

"Well, chat away then. You can start by telling me your name at least. You seem to know mine already."

"It's Malcolm. I'm sorry. I didn't intend to startle you. I asked Zuri for your name."

"He's a right little busybody, isn't he? Wait till I get my hands on him. But he's not Cilla Black, and this isn't an episode of 'Blind Date' either."

Malcolm liked it better when Danni smiled. It seemed to soften her edges a little. Taking her lead, he said,

"No, it can't be a blind date, can it? We've already met. But I wonder if you would consider going on an actual one with me?"

"You seem like a nice bloke, Malcolm. But you see, the thing is, I'm not interested in dating anyone at the moment."

"Ok, I get it. You don't find me attractive. Fair enough. But would you consider just going out with me as friends? Most Saturday nights I go line dancing at Jesters nightclub. It's a real laugh. It attracts all sorts. If nothing else, I can promise you that you'll have fun. "

"Oh, yes, I've heard of that old flea pit. Wasn't it quite popular in the sixties and seventies? My mother told me that all the big stars performed there," Danni replied whilst realising they had struck up a conversation together.

"Yes, that's the one. So will you go with me then, please? I'm not very good at the moves, though. I've got the coordination of Dumbo on ice, but no one cares, to be honest."

It was cruel to make the poor bloke wait any longer than she had to. As she quickly weighed up his offer, she noticed his green and brown flecked eyes twinkling at her. When she thought about it, Malcolm seemed harmless enough. It'd been a long time since she had done anything more than work and mope about with her friends. So maybe a change was as good as a rest. "Go on then, I'll come with you. Curiosity has killed the cat. But just as friends though, let's make that clear."

"Yes, just as friends, that's fine by me. I'll meet you here at seven next Saturday night. Right, I have an early start in the morning, so please excuse me. I'm a long-distance lorry driver, and I need to get to Glasgow and back tomorrow." Malcolm left the pub feeling a little taller than he did when he entered.

Danni returned to our table. She looked baffled. Carla and Christian nudged us, but kept quiet. But I just couldn't help diving in with my size eleven feet. I said, "Danni, what was all that about? From where we were sitting, it looked like that man was trying to chat you up. The poor fool."

"To be completely honest, I've no idea what went on. And to make matters worse, I've agreed to go line dancing with him. But only as friends, though."

"You, line dancing? And with a stranger? No."

"I know. I just felt so sorry for him standing there like a chip waiting for vinegar. And let's be honest, I'm not the most approachable of women. He's brave for having a go. Few men catch me off guard, but his kind green eyes mesmerised me. It was that or I've had too many sherbets."

There was just one thing on my mind. I leaned over, made a prayer sign with my hands and said, "Do we need to buy a new hat yet?"

It was amazing what Danni kept in the back of her closet. As a parting gift, Miss Nancy Eclair had each given Max, Wayne, and Danni a cast-off dress. As Nancy wiped the tears away from under her beaded lashes, the last thing she said to the three of them was, "Just squeeze it and think of me from time to time, will you?" And then she turned on her gilded heel and headed for the lights of the big cities.

But Danni never realised just how useful her cowgirl gingham dress was going to be. After a few nips and tucks in all the right places, it fitted like a glove. Well, that is, if it was a sequined glove with a netted underwire. She was well and truly in touch with her inner drag queen. But this was something more. It was so comforting to slip into a dress that reminded her of Miss Nancy Eclair and her Jack doing their 'Dolly and Kenny' number on the bar. She looked in the hallway mirror, turned from side to side, mumbled, and dropped her shoulders. Luckily, no one had spotted her leaving the house before she tittered the familiar path to the 'Potters Arms'. Her patent black leather boots were killing her, but that wasn't going to stop her from making the most of her evening. She took a deep breath, pulled her dress down and her boots up, and swung the boozer's door open. Before it had as much as creaked shut, a wolf whistle startled her.

"Yee haw, slapper-my-thigh. Look fellas, if it isn't our very own Calamity Jane without the pigtails. Have you just blown in from the Windy City? Come on Doris, give us a song while you are waiting for your secret love to arrive," Simon blurted from behind the bar, to everyone's amusement.

"Just shut your gob, pour me a pint and get back onto your deadwood stage!"

Someone was well and truly taking the wet now. That bloody song was playing. *Islands in the stream, that is what we ar*e. She hadn't heard it at first. *No one in between, how can we be wrong?* But now some kind soul had turned up the jukebox. *Sail away with me to another world.* Dolly's and Kenny's dulcet tones drifted over the pub and sliced through her heart again. *And we rely on each other, ah ha.* It still hurt so much. *From one lover to another, ah-ha.* Thank god, that Jack couldn't see her dressed like a cast-off from a drag show. She wouldn't have lived that one down. He would've had years' worth of material to embarrass her with at any given drunken moment. If only.

Thank goodness Malc had arrived. He winked, took off his cream Stetson, bowed and said in perhaps the worst attempt at an American accent she had ever heard, "Well, howdy, partner. Y'all as pretty as a peach, Darlin."

She didn't know whether to feel flattered or insulted, but laughed all the same. He'd pulled his light brown mullet back into a tight ponytail. With the hair removed from his brow, Danni could properly study the kindness in his eyes as they chatted at the bar. As she eyed him up, she realised he was quite handsome in a rough rodeo sort of way. He tucked his paisley red neckerchief into a crisp black shirt that had white tassels on the fringe. He wore a heavily embossed black leather belt which sported a tarnished silver ornate buckle. A pair of healed cowboy boots complimented his skin-tight black jeans. This extra inch or so was just enough to stop her from towering over him. He was no Doctor John Stokes, but this wasn't necessarily a bad thing. After all, just look where that had got her. Yes, the more she talked to Malcolm, the more she realised he was like a comfy pair of slippers rather than a pair of painful boots. With a final grin from Simon and Zuri, it was time for the couple to mosey on out of the boozer and to Jester's nightclub. Instead of having a white stallion tied up outside, they got into a black cab.

"You're such a gentleman, thank you," Danni said as he opened the cab door and then stumbled in behind her.

"Oh my goodness, I'm sorry. I didn't mean to sit on you."

Danni laughed, ran her hand up his leg and said, "Please don't apologise Malc, I'm fine. I'm a lot tougher than I look." But neither one of them moved until they arrived at the club.

Every Saturday night, a cyclone scooped up the Jester and dropped it into Nashville, just like Dorothy's house in The Wizard of Oz. Country twangs rang out above the amethyst glow that filled the auditorium. Danni awkwardly followed her date to a round table on the edge of the dance floor. That netted underskirt chaffed on her thighs like a cheese grater. Malcolm adjusted the purple table lamp, dusted the cobweb off the shade, and pulled the worn velvet seat out from under the table. A plume of dust escaped into the glow as he wiped off the rickety seat with his hat. "I'm sorry, this place has seen better days." I've been coming here for years. They aren't spending any money on it. It's hard to believe now, but in its heyday in the sixties and seventies, all the headliners played here.

"The likes of Cliff Richard and Cilla Black were regulars. It's hard to believe, but even Roy Orbison sang here. Sadly, the only thing that is running scared now are the club's owners. The council want to knock it down and build a multi-storey carpark.

"Sadie would be turning in her grave if she only knew. That old girl was beautiful from the inside out. She'd worked here for years, pandering to the celebrities' every need. When my parents brought me down here as a teenager, she took a real shine to me. It wasn't long before she had taught me how to line dance. It's never been the same without her."

"No, I like it here. Thank you for sharing your lovely story with me. It's such a small world, isn't it? I knew of Sadie through her daughter Carla. Yes, it was such a pity when she died. Carla was in pieces for a long time. They say that the good ones go first, don't they? She's a nurse and also a very close friend of mine. Funnily enough, she was sitting with her husband, Christian, in our group of friends the very night that you asked me out. They've just got married and returned from their honeymoon."

"Well, I never. It certainly is a small world. I had no idea," Malcolm replied.

"Carla will be over the moon when I tell her about this and your connection with Sadie. Who would've thought it?"

And it was true: Danni loved the club. It wasn't trying to pretend to be anything that it wasn't. She saw the genuine looks of happiness on people's faces as they got up and line danced to a bit of Achy Breaky Heart. Without thinking about it, she soon got whisked into the purple haze and did her best to keep up with Malcolm as they danced to the rhythm of the Watermelon Crawl. Now and again she caught his eyes, which sparkled under the reflection of a disco ball. The atmosphere of the entire club changed from hoedown to a meandering stroll under a Nashville moon. She could almost hear the distant honky tonk and smell the heavy bourbon in the air as a singer was announced from over a cracked speaker. Like a poor man's George Strait, the act swaggered to centre stage, sat on a bar stool in a single spotlight and said,

"Good evening ladies and gentlemen, it's a real pleasure to be with you all tonight again. For those of you who don't know me, I'm Mark

Nightingale. It's awesome to have your company. I sure hope you enjoy my set."

Danni and Malc watched from their table together. Mark tipped his black Stetson to the audience, positioned the red guitar against his white embroidered shirt, and sang in one of the deepest and most heartfelt voices that Danni had heard for a long time. Like a moth to the flame, couples drifted to the dance floor to soak up the romance of the singers' seductive tones. Malc cleared his throat, glanced over at Danni and said,

"I know that this isn't strictly a date, but would you like to dance?"

"I'd love to, thank you, kind sir."

Malc took his date by his large hands and gently led her to the dance floor to join the others. She didn't seem bothered by his hand on her back. She felt his warm breath on her face as his rib cage moved slowly up and down. As they danced, she couldn't help noticing that Malcolm was whispering along to the words as Mark sang. *I know you loved him a long time ago. Even now in my arms, you still want him I know. But darling this time let your memories die. When you hold me tonight don't close your eyes.* He gently guided her into a twirl, and as she faced him again, Malc sang, "Don't close your eyes, it's me, not some fantasy. Darling, just once let yesterday go and you'll find more love than you've ever known. Just hold me tight when you love me tonight and don't close your eyes."

So she didn't. Instead, she leaned in and kissed the man who was standing directly in front of her. At that moment, she realised she wasn't lost anymore. Danni could've eaten the hind legs off a scabby donkey and even gone back for seconds as they left the Jester arm in arm. All of this romance had triggered her appetite. And Malc was more than happy to oblige in any way he could to satisfy her every desire.

"I know just the place. It's so romantic and the food is amazing. We'll find a little table at the back of the restaurant. Only the best will do for you," Malc said as he squeezed her hand tightly. He still couldn't believe his luck. How had he broken down Danni's defences so quickly? When would she wake up and realise that it was all a terrible mistake?

They just arrived at their destination before the heavens opened. The smell of freshly cooked food was intoxicating as they closed the steamed door behind them. Danni warmed her hand over the stainless steel countertop of the open kitchen as they headed to the seating. The food smelt divine and was all freshly cooked to order. Even though the place was full, they were able to find a table for two at the rear of the restaurant. The more that she glanced down the menu, the more her stomach gurgled. But luckily, her rumbling went unnoticed because of the sound of the culinary delights that were being prepared within spitting distance of her. A plump waitress in a pink checked housecoat and hairnet came over, produced a damp rag from her pocket, and wiped the Formica top clean. From her breast pocket, the woman produced a soiled notebook. Through her cracked teeth, she cackled,

"Well, duck, what do yer want? Just to let yer know, we've a special on a cod supper with double-fried battered chips and large mushy peas if you're hungry. Oh, and it includes a mug of tea or coffee, too."

Danni looked up at the waitress and squinted. It was difficult to see her properly under the glow of the luminescent blue fly trap. She looked at her date, who was busy drawing love hearts on the greasy tabletop, laughed, and said,

"That sounds perfect. We'll have two large fish and chip suppers. Can I have plenty of vinegar on mine, please?"

# Chapter Four

George worked his last day at the City Infirmary and left to customary cheers of 'he's a jolly good fellow' ringing from the medical and nursing fraternity. He had retired from his job as a consultant oncologist and could finally cut the ball and chain that he had been carrying around for all of these years. As he pulled up, his double bay-fronted Victorian pile looked nothing more than a glorified prison. Perfectly clipped box hedging lined a raked gravel path. Two topiary guards stood to attention as he fumbled for the key to his cell. It had been a long time since fuchsia bushes had wildly welcomed him home. But today was different. He didn't feel the familiar taste of acid burning his throat as the door swung to welcome him into this musty hell. He could still smell the essence of moth-coated menace hanging in the air, whether or not his wife was there. But now he didn't care anymore what she thought or what she did. She could line the path with pink triangles with his face stuck on them for all he cared. He never forgot the names she called him the night he got arrested. But every dog has its day. She had no collateral to control him with anymore. Jack had sadly died and Christian was happily married. He was just plain old George Taylor with the rest of his life in front of him. Well, sixty was the new forty after all.

It didn't take long for him to pack his bags and wait for Maria to return from visiting Christian. Clomp. The familiar weight of her rattled through the front door as she dropped her Prada handbag on the Minton tiles. Only the best was good enough for her. But this time, her entrance didn't fill him with dread. Clatter. She stomped in her hideous brogues through the kitchen door. Just had she had done for many years. She flicked the switch to the kettle, sighed and plonked her ripples down on a chair opposite him. George sat still. He didn't get up and make her an instant coffee. Day after day, week after week, month after month, year after year, and decade after decade, he had to resist the urge to spit secretly in her brew as he made it. But today was different. Instead of jumping up, he buried his head in his paper, ignoring her wobbling the table with her stomach as she caught it. From the comfort of his newspaper, he slowly hummed the tune of 'Maria' from Westside Story until it filled the gap between them. He only stopped when she ripped the paper from his hands and hissed from her blubbering jowls. This serenade marked his final gift to the woman who had controlled and abused him throughout his life in the name of decency and respectability. And he had let her. But not anymore. They were done. He grabbed his bags, hidden just beyond the back door, handed her a brown envelope containing his divorce solicitor's information, and vanished before she could react.

George drank his first black tea. He couldn't open the annoying plastic carton of milk that sat on the saucer. What sadistic bastard had invented them? He wasn't going to ask the waitress for help. What would she think? By the second cup, his hands had stopped shaking long enough for him to pierce the carton. He sat quietly, watching the world go by, and guarded his two suitcases that were stored on a trolley next to him. When his train was announced, he slowly pushed the trolley to his carriage. Luckily, a young man with a chiselled face and muscular arms kindly carried the cases onto the train for him. George closed his eyes and let out a quiet sigh when the stationmaster's whistle blew his old life out and the train chugged away. The man sat opposite him at the table of four seats. When George opened his eyes, he saw the man frowning at him. He said,

"Are you OK Sir?"

"Thank you, I am now."

"Please call me Harry, sir. I was worried about you. You appeared on the verge of passing out before I grabbed your bags. Are you sure that you are OK? Here, have my bag of wine gums. It's better than nothing. Have you eaten?"

"Thank you, Harry. No, come to think of it, I haven't," George replied whilst chewing on the sweets. "You're very kind. Please call me George. 'Sir' makes me feel even older than I am."

By the time George had eaten an overpriced bacon and cheese bap and swigged two further corrugated cardboard cups of something that masqueraded as tea, his headache had disappeared and he relaxed. He smiled at the exuberance of youth that sat opposite, waving his biceps and scratching his black goatee as they chatted. It turned out that Harry was off to London to visit his boyfriend who worked as a musical theatre actor in the West End. All of this information just tumbled out of his thick lips without as much as a second thought. Plumping out his chest, he said,

"He's in Phantom at the moment. I never tire of seeing him in that show. Despite knowing it will happen, my heart nearly stops when the chandelier swings towards the audience. It's a fab show. Have you seen it?"

"No, I haven't, but I love the music. I almost choke when I hear Sarah Brightman sing 'Think of Me' I've heard it a lot at my old job."

"Sorry, me and my big mouth. I have spoiled the start of the show for you now. What do you mean? Were you a singer or something?" Harry asked.

"No, I used to work at a hospital before I retired. Sadly, this song is quite popular at funerals."

"Well, what brings you to the big city? Are you having a holiday?"

George shook his head and sipped another mouthful of sludge. "That's a fantastic question, Harry. Once I've figured it out, you'll be the first to know. The only thing I'm sure of is there's no turning back. And for now, that is as far as it goes."

"Well, mystery man, that's fine by me." Harry said whilst scribbling down a telephone number on a paper serviette and shoving it in George's top pocket of his tweed jacket. "Here is my number. If you ever need someone to buy you wine gums or to ruin the opening of a musical for you, then please call me. London can be a lonely place and it is easy to get lost here."

"Bless you, thank you, Harry."

And then it hit him. This young gay man was kind and had given compassion to a total stranger. George grabbed hold of his stomach. What kind of monster had he been? Before Jack had left for the RAF, he had ignored his silent plea for help that bellowed from his bedroom on a constant loop. That bloody song still cut him like a knife whenever he heard it. *One day the boy decided to let them know the way he felt inside.* Why did he walk past Jack's bedroom door? It was too late now. *He couldn't stand to hide it, his mother, she broke down and cried.* What had he done? *Oh my father, why don't you talk to me now?* If only he could speak to Jack once more and apologise. But no, he had put the last nail in his coffin and called him a filthy sodomite. *Oh my mother, do you still cry yourself to sleep? Are you still proud of your little boy?* He stood by Maria as she thrust a wedge of money into their son's pocket as he spat hatred at him. He could still hear those last words echo in his head. And it came true, Jack did drop dead. *Don't be afraid, love will mend your broken wings. Time will slip away. Learn to be brave.*

And it wasn't only Jack that had to learn to be brave. Who would have thought that the same song would ring his arrival in London? *Far from home now, waiting by the telephone. There's a new world, you can make it on your own.*

George felt a hairy hand brush his palm as Harry grabbed the suitcases. They stood by the door and waited to jump onto the platform. "Are you sure you're OK? You were miles away. I thought you were going to have a wine-gum moment again."

"My apologies. I was just thinking about my children. I must call Christian and his new wife. I didn't exactly plan this trip and left without as much as a goodbye. They'll be worried."

"Well, as long as you are OK. Let me help you off the train and carry your cases till we get to the entrance, at least. I'm sure this platform gets longer each time I visit," Harry shouted over the din of faceless passengers and the smell of London life.

A tall, broad man with glossy brown hair and the whitest teeth that George had ever seen was waiting for Harry at the station entrance. It was easy to imagine this stud in a dress shirt and black tails belting out 'Music of the Night'. But he wasn't singing now or wearing a white mask. Instead, he scooped Harry into his firm grip and kissed him. In that tender moment, George vanished and escaped down the escalator before Harry realised he was gone.

Watching the vermin scurry on the underground track took him right back to his childhood. But now was no time for another pity party down memory lane as he joined the sea of people competing for standing room only on the tube. He needed to keep his wits about him if he was going to navigate through the sweat-infused crowd. Luckily, it wasn't long before he had reached his destination. Until he could find the time to set up shop properly, he had cleverly booked into one of those functional but soulless chains of hotels that had been breeding like rabbits all over the country. He may have been desperate to leave Maria, but he wasn't stupid. The last thing he wanted was to be trailing around London on speck, looking for a stable for the night to lay his greying locks.

George arrived at his destination following a couple of line changes. Luckily, he had avoided the Pied Piper for now as he resurfaced at Putney Bridge. Fantasising about his plans had kept him going. He never imagined they would become reality. Amidst Maria's madness, he'd meticulously planned for this day. In the meantime, he settled for the conference circuit and his research assistant, Colin. But George knew his assistant was only interested in one thing and one thing only. He wanted to ride on his reputation as a prominent oncologist to get to the top and would do anything with anyone to get there. And for more years than George was willing to admit, he had let him. Well, the road to hell had to be paid for in one way or another. Nothing was for nothing.

He found a public phone box that, unfortunately, smelt of pee. But this didn't stop him from standing and staring at the receiver for a while before picking it up. After all, it wasn't the first time he had stood in public urine. If he didn't phone his son, they would send out a search party. He didn't want to worry Christian and Carla any more than he needed to. George wiped the phone, inserted a coin, breathed deeply, and dialled his son's number. It was time to come clean - well, almost. Luckily, Christian answered after a couple of rings. George said,

"Hello Christian, it's your father. I'm calling you from a public phone box in London, so I need to keep it short. There's no easy way to say this, so I'm just going to spit it out. I've left your mother; we're divorcing. We haven't been getting on for a very long time. Now that I've finally retired, I have plucked up the courage and have left her.

It's not her fault though, it's mine. Please don't blame her. We want different things out of life, that's all.

I'll come back from time to time. I won't miss the birth of my first grandchild for anything. Did you hear me, Christian?"

Christian heard his father put another coin in the slot. "Yes, Dad, I heard you. To be completely honest, I can't say that I am entirely surprised. I remember how things were at home. I don't want that for my child. It was like stepping on eggshells most of my childhood. Jack and I hated it. If Mum and you can't be happy together, then you deserve a crack at it separately."

George felt a few wet tears hit the phone. "I love you, Christian. I haven't said it for a very long time, but I really do. I'm so sorry for everything."

"And I love you too, Dad. Just look after yourself and keep in touch. Let us know once you are straight. Goodbye for now."

George put down the receiver, picked up a card for a local property agent and sighed as he rescued his two suitcases from the phone box floor. Maybe he was imagining it, but they didn't seem as heavy as before. His accommodation was only a few steps from the phone box, anyway. He checked into the hotel, went to his room, threw off his shoes and sank face down on the bed. For the first time in many years, George fell soundly asleep.

# Chapter Five

Ali sniffed his armpits and decided that it was time for a shower. Stale sweat and spent Brut was not the smell that he was going for; even if Harry Cooper told him to just 'splash it all over'. The hot jets felt good against his firm skin and long black locks. As he sat, stretched and lathered, his mind wandered to the day ahead. With a bit of luck, he'd bump into that lovely young doctor and strike up a conversation. But it was almost, but not entirely, impossible to flirt over a greasy Bain Marie. A hairnet, chef's whites and smelling of chip fat weren't the best pulling gear. There was something he liked about this man. In between the splatter of suds against the wet room floor and the mounting steam, Ali closed his eyes and bit his bottom lip. He had a thing for men with Northern accents. This man looked cute as a button in that oversized doctor's coat, shiny black shoes and a crisp white shirt with a blue tie. He fantasised about climbing over the counter, ripping off his clothes there and then, and doing unspeakable things to his swimmer's physique. But that would get them both the sack. Damm it, where had the time gone? He towel-dried the fuzz of black hair that covered every inch of him, rubbed roll-on under his arms, did as Henry Cooper had instructed and plotted his next move. He quickly dressed and rushed to work before his hospital kitchen shift. Nothing dampens the ardour like preparing an industrial batch of semolina pudding for the lunchtime rush.

Dylan felt like a fish out of water in the big hospital. In the heat of the moment, he had left the comfort of the City Infirmary. Enough was enough. George had messed with his head for the last time. Dylan cringed as he thought about his dishevelled lover's hollers begging him to stay. He could still smell that rancid piss as he stormed off, leaving George with his trousers soaking on the cubicle floor. It took every fibre in his tattered heart to turn and run. He couldn't stand back and watch the man he loved marry Maria. That was just too twisted. So here he was, footloose and fancy-free. The easy part was landing a junior doctor's job in this large London Hospital. Living with what he had done was an entirely different matter. Why had he been so cruel? There were better ways to say goodbye than with a farewell fuck. Even George didn't deserve this.

Dylan sauntered into the staff canteen, still deep in his thoughts. He grabbed a plastic tray and joined the queue of hungry battery hens. A chef had caught his attention on a few occasions. Whilst he had made polite conversation, he wasn't sure if he was ready to jump from the cubicle and into the frying pan just yet. But this man was persistent and couldn't look any more different from George. His chef's whites could hardly contain his broad shoulders and long legs. As he moved down the line, he wondered what this goliath would look like once released from his rather unflattering hairnet. Their eyes locked for longer than anything that was socially acceptable for passing over a plate of chips, egg and sausage.

Ali made his first move. Their fingertips touched as he passed Dylan the hot plate. He felt himself smiling from ear to ear as he said,

"Hi- Hi there, be careful with that. I don't want you to drop your food. A young strapping lad like yourself needs all the fuel he can get. It must be tough on those wards. Sorry, I didn't catch your name?"

"My name is Dylan."

"I'm Ali. I can't talk now or I'll get lynched. Can we meet tonight? Sorry to be so direct. I get off at six," he said before causing a traffic jam.

Without having the time to wriggle out of it, Dylan said, "Okay then, you have twisted my arm. There is a pub across from the hospital. I can meet you there if you want." And with that, he moved on down the line to pay for his food, feeling a little happier than he had in ages.

"What is it? Can you tell me where it hurts?" Dylan asked whilst grabbing hold of the lady's withered hands. Getting a complete history from a patient who lacked awareness of their name, location, or reason for being admitted was always difficult. She was wandering the streets close to the hospital when they found her, wearing nothing more than a nightie and a pair of wet, sloppy slippers. The stained nightdress had welded to her skin. Luckily, the police had picked her up and brought her into the Accident and Emergency Department before god knows what could happen to her. A local restaurant owner had found her rummaging through his bins, looking for food in the back alley of his kebab shop. She still had the remnants of decaying meat on her breath as two burly porters wheeled her into an admission cubicle. Bin juice and decay slathered her long grey wispy hair. Dylan was determined to get to the heart of the problem, despite her confusion trying to stop him. All those years at medical school had prepared him for this. He would systematically examine his patient, formulate a differential diagnosis, and make a plan. It was child's play, with or without a comprehensive history. The old bird probably had a water infection causing a delirium. It was more than likely that she'd got dementia, anyway. It would be a quick call to the Geri's and off she would toddle for them to sort her out. Whilst half holding his breath, he leaned over her to get a better look at what was happening. He looked into her empty eyes and mimicked pain. "Does it hurt?"

The lady rattled the cot's sides and retreated further up the bed. It was impossible; he was getting nowhere fast. Oh well, if she wouldn't let him near her, then what could he do? He scribbled something in her notes and left his patient to phone the older adults ward. Just as he was about to pick up the receiver, his cavalry arrived in the form of Sister Grace Jackson. Her friends called her Grace, but junior doctors who were unfortunately posted to her emergency department referred to her as Sister Jackson. Tutting at Dylan, she adjusted her glasses, retrieved her silver buckle from under her bosom, and took over. She put her arm around the lady. "What is it, precious? Come here, let me help you, darling. You poor thing, you look famished. You're all skin and bones. Let's get you nice and clean and some sustenance into you, eh? Then this doctor over here can have a little look at you."

Grace left the cubicle to get food for the lady, glaring at the doctor who was getting under her feet. Raising her eyebrows to almost the same height as her pinned beehive, she cleared her throat and said,

"Don't they teach you any compassion up north? Can't you see how scared the poor soul is? Goodness me, she's a lady and not a diagnosis. Now sit, hold her hand and talk to her whilst I find a bowl of something hot. And then we'll take it from there."

He was stunned into submission. The only words he could find were, "Yes, Sister, of course."

She returned ten minutes later with a bowl of hot porridge to find Dylan doing what she had told him to do. Sister Jackson clasped the bowl in her hands and offered the lady a spoon. She looked blankly at it but moved her head towards the bowl. Sister Jackson then retrieved the spoon, mixed the porridge, and fed the lady. In almost a whisper, she said,

"Here you are, my precious. Don't you worry, let Gracie help you."

Dylan watched in awe. This simple act was far more than a bowl of porridge. And as much as he was ashamed to admit it, she was right. His bedside manner had left the building. But never again. He stroked the lady's emaciated hand as Sister Jackson fed and soothed her from the other side of the bed. Whilst this poor soul couldn't understand in words, she responded to the unspoken kindness. Sister Jackson smiled at her and said,

"Oh, you poor sparrow, you needed that, didn't you? Shall we ask our doctor here to leave us whilst we have a little wash? You'll feel much better in a lovely clean nightie, won't you precious? We'll invite him back when we girls have had a bit of privacy, shall we?"

But, despite her best efforts, Grace didn't wash the patient. Whilst the lady was still half-dressed in a hospital gown, she called Dylan back into the cubicle. He could see where Sister Jackson had cut the lady's rancid nightie away from her. But no, it wasn't only the bin swill that had been hanging in the air. She raised her eyebrows for the second time during this consultation and removed the white towel that had been covering the lady's torso. It took every ounce of what was left of Dylan's bedside manner to keep calm. He may've been inexperienced, but this was an easy diagnosis. The sight of a fungating breast tumour growing through a nightgown was sadly unmistakable. This was going to take far more than a bed bath to put right. And they still didn't even know her name.

After comforting the lady and calling the oncologists, they took a five-minute break behind the central nursing station together. Dylan felt a firm hand on his shoulder as Sister Jackson handed him a cup of tea. "Are you alright Doctor? We see all sorts here, but you never get used to it."

"How long had that lady been wandering? Anything could have happened to her. She's got cancer, for Christ's sake, and I missed it. I was so wrong. She must've been in agony."

"I know. It's tragic, isn't it? You see, these streets aren't lined with gold. It breaks my old heart. Just listen to your nursing staff and you won't go far wrong. We're a team, remember. Don't beat yourself up. None of us are perfect. Please call me Grace."

"Thank you, Grace, you're very kind. I'm Dylan," he replied whilst taking the last swig from his plastic cup. A buzzer rang in the next casualty, and this unlikely pair jumped to their feet again.

---

This boozer was certainly a far cry from the Potters Arms. Dylan swallowed hard, wiped his mouth and stopped to admire the frontage. Wooden picnic tables enticed him to the double-fronted entrance. Someone had painted every bench black and placed a golden parasol and matching ashtray on each one. He looked up and clocked a row of smart brass lamps punctuating the gilded signage. On either side, large bay windows framed a glossy black door. Was this a pub or one of those swanky high-end London hotel lobbies? It could've even been an exclusive gentleman's club. Once through the door, he stopped, fidgeted with the lapel to his brown corduroy jacket, and tucked his red lumberjack shirt into his blue bell-bottom jeans. This place was even better on the inside. If he wasn't careful, then the till in a place like this could easily swallow all of his meagre wages. A quartet of gilded chandeliers presided over a plethora of studded black circular leather booths. Ornate stained-glass windows depicting London landmarks encased each booth. Scattered between them were a series of dark wooden tables and winged-back leather chairs. A central aisle led to a bar that stretched from one side of the room to the other. Smartly polished beer pumps stood to attention on the dark wooden top. Bar staff with slicked hair, crisp white shirts and stiff black waistcoats stood in front of a myriad of spirits that floated from glass shelves. A series of arched bar-to-ceiling mirrors provided a backdrop for the entire room. These engraved masterpieces gave the illusion of making the pub look even larger than it was. A tall, slender man who wore black eyeliner flashed his teeth at Dylan and said in a deep voice,

"Welcome to Gatsby's Bar. What will it be, governor?"

Dylan was a child in a sweet shop. Even a northern lad could recognise that this place was something more than your average boozer. At some point, he intended to work along the pumps. "I'll have a pint of lager and lime for now, please."

The barman smiled and poured a frothing pint of liquid relief. Dylan slid into a luxurious booth by the door. Through the stained glass, he noticed shadows of friends talking and laughing. He pushed the pangs of regret to the back of his head. But he had made his soggy bed and now he had no choice but to lie in it. He sighed, gulped his drink, and tapped his fingers. Without thinking about it, he played along to the rhythm of Rod Stewart on his tabletop piano. Just before someone passed him a candelabra, his date interrupted him. "Hi Dylan, good to see you. Thank you for coming. Let me get you a refill. What are you drinking?"

"Oh, erm, sorry, I didn't recognise you with your clothes on, so to speak. Hello Ali. A pint of lager and lime please, if you don't mind."

Dylan kicked himself. He was an idiot. Of course, the man would look different out of his hair net and chef's whites. Ali strode slowly over to the bar. There was no doubt he filled his pale blue Levis in all the right places. Just as Dylan had suspected, his date's long legs went all the way up to his firm buttocks. And now he could see those lovely, long black glossy locks hanging over his broad shoulders, almost touching his slender waistline. As Ali turned around from the bar, Dylan looked away. It was rude to stare, even if his front was as impressive as his rear.

Ali squeaked across the soft leather until the men were almost touching their thighs. He took off his navy denim jacket to reveal a ribbed white t-shirt. A lucky thick red stripe wrapped around his pecs. Ali smiled and looked Dylan in the eyes. "Thank you for agreeing to meet me. Believe it or not, it's been a while since I've been out. I spend most of my evenings in the hospital gym, as it's close to my ground-floor room. But look at me babbling on, sorry."

"Hang on a minute, so you're living in the staff accommodation block, then. I'm on the tenth floor. I wish I'd known. All this time, I've been technically sleeping on top of you." He smirked and continued, "Since coming to London, I haven't got out much either. There's my work, and that's about it. Wandering up West is boring when you've no one to share it with. People just don't stop and pass the time of day here."

Ali casually rubbed his thigh until it accidentally on purpose touched his date's leg. "Yes, I guess you've been topping me for a while. And unfortunately, I didn't feel a damn thing. What brought you here?"

"Love, I'm afraid. It's not what you think, though. I came here to escape a man who was never mine to keep," he said before realising that he had broken the golden rule of dating, "oh, sorry, you don't want to hear about all of this."

"No, go on, if you want to tell me, then I'm more than happy to hear it. And for the record, this man was a bloody fool. I would never let someone like you go."

Dylan sighed, realising that he was already halfway down his second pint, and then said, "George and I met whilst we were teenagers. But it was very complicated. I had to leave him in the end. He finally made his choice and married. I couldn't watch George and Maria play happy families. It just broke my heart."

"Right, I see. That's painful. That would send anyone over the edge, but it's his loss and my gain."

"Well, you're not backward at coming forward, are you, Ali?"

"I've been trying to speak to you since you got here, Doctor Dylan. I don't want to scare you off, but I like you. There, I've said it. Life is too short for regrets."

"No, I like the fact that you're direct and to the point. I know exactly where I stand," Dylan said whilst running his hand up his date's leg, "and if you play your cards right, there won't be ten floors between us tonight."

Dylan wanted to kiss the succulent pair of lips that framed Ali's black goatee until he got beard burn. He imagined running his hand down the side of his date's face until it cupped his firm buttocks. The desire to taste every inch of this man's body consumed him. The scent of their bodies entwined in shared sweat was almost tangible. He could almost smell their heat and feel the weight of Ali's legs wrapped tightly around his waist. And then Dylan shuddered and stopped fantasising before he couldn't stand up and go to the bar. It was his round, and he was already a pint ahead of Ali. Dylan returned from the bar with a pint of lager for Ali and a sensible soft drink for himself. After all, he was a two-pint kind of a guy at the best of times, but even more so if he was on a promise. Ali had gone from a confident wildebeest to a jellyfish in the time it had taken Dylan to return with the drinks. He sat with his head in his hands and those beautiful black locks now covering his face.

"What is it? Are you OK? Are you ill? Please tell me what's wrong, I'm worried," Dylan said whilst rubbing his dates-shaking shoulder, "have I said something wrong?"

"No, it's not you, you're perfect, it's me. I need to tell you something."

"You're scaring me now. What is it? Please tell me!" He was now attracting a little attention from a few passing strangers.

Ali wiped the tears that were dripping from his long eyelashes and looked towards the floor. "I'm sorry, but I've been lying to you and you don't deserve that, especially after everything that you've told me. I've been playing with you and leading you on. But to tell you the truth, I've been acting. I've no confidence at all. These muscles and my long hair are just a camouflage to hide who I am deep down."

"What do you mean, Ali? Who are you? I'm so confused", Dylan said whilst thanking his lucky stars that he hadn't had a third pint.

"Men have gone running for the hills once they know what's wrong with me. Not one of them could accept me for who I am."

"Whatever it is, I want to help you," Dylan replied with his arm now firmly around his date's shoulder.

"I have an above-left knee amputee. I wear a prosthesis. Does that bother you?"

He slid his finger under Ali's chin and lifted his face until they made eye-to-eye contact. Pain seeped from his shaking body. "No, absolutely not. Why would it? You're the most beautiful man that I've ever seen. It's brave of you to tell me this. It only makes me like you more. I want to know everything about you."

"You're the first man who has seen past my amputee. I'm so pleased that I plucked up the courage and asked you out. Getting a date has been the easy part, but that's as far as it has gone in the past."

"Please don't put me on a pedestal. I get things wrong all the time. Trust me on that one," Dylan replied.

By now, the men were almost sitting on top of each other in the booth. It was easy to chat with everything out on the table. Now and again, Dylan purposely touched both of his date's legs as they put the world to rights. Ali cringed as Dylan confessed that Sister Gladys Jackson had rescued him when he had got things so wrong earlier in the day. He laughed and reassured him that everyone knew Gladys had a bark worse than her bite. A heart of gold beat under her starched pinny and navy blue dress. Even when bigots and bullies racially abused her, she always kept her cool. Some people were just cruel. Since the likes of 'Love Thy Neighbour' and 'Rising Damp' blasted out of TV sets every week, society had deemed it acceptable to laugh at people who didn't fit the same white cookie cutter mould. Ali explained that if it was sauce for the ITV gooses, then it was sauce for racist ganders too. They believed they had a God-given right to call Sister Jackson vile names if they weren't getting their way in the busy accident and emergency department. And it was just the same for homophobes too. If society could laugh at characters like Dick Emery's 'Clarence' or John Inman's 'Mr Humphries', they would always perceive gay people as nothing more than circus sideshow freaks. Dylan sat quietly and listened to his date open up his heart. Whilst sipping the dregs from the bottom of his pint glass, he said that being gay, disabled and from the Indian culture hadn't exactly won him any popularity contests either. If you are constantly called a 'Paki, faggot Flid' at school for long enough, there becomes a turning point when you believe it.

But Dylan didn't believe this any more than he thought that his date was unworthy of love. They left the pub, walking arm-in-arm. A cool wind blew through the parasols and the familiar smell of passing traffic soon replaced the allure of beer. Dylan blinked as the number seventy-three hurled past him. The din of constant traffic was taking some getting used to. He could walk from the City Infirmary to the Potter's Arms in comparative peace and hardly bump into a soul. But that was then, and this was now. And more to the point, there was never a handsome stud linking him back home. George wouldn't be caught dead showing affection in public. He smiled and rested his arm on the small of Ali's back as they crossed the road. Maybe this London lark wasn't as bad as he thought it was going to be. Within ten minutes, the men were outside of their accommodation block. Dylan broke the awkward silence between them first. He turned to Ali and said,

"I've enjoyed your company tonight. You're a lovely man and I'm lucky to have met you. Can we do it again sometime, please?"

They shared the same breath and moved closer to each other. Ali's eyes said it all. He couldn't hide the fact that he was smitten with Dylan. He pulled him even closer. "I can't think of anything better. I've been lonely for too long,"

Within five minutes, they were hovering around the door to Ali's room, wondering what to do next. Ali had mentioned his inexperience, and Dylan didn't want to pressurise him or make him uncomfortable. To his utter amazement, Ali cleared his throat and said,

"Would you like to come in for a while? I'm not ready to say goodnight just yet. "

"Of course, I'd love to, but just to let you know that I'll go at your speed. There's no pressure from me."

The room was very similar to Dylan's. In the corner was a single framed pine bed. Opposite was a matching wardrobe and set of draws. Dylan saw photos on the dresser and a crutch by the wardrobe door. The room smelt wonderful; it was a concentrated version of Ali himself. Dylan breathed in deeply as Ali turned off the overhead fluorescent strip light in favour of the bedside lamp. As Dylan's eyes adjusted to the far more relaxing peach glow, he sat on the bed whilst Ali switched on the kettle. In a few minutes, both men were sitting side by side on the bed together, slurping tea and wondering what to do next. Once halfway down the mug, Ali said,

"I've wanted to kiss you since the moment I saw you in the canteen a few weeks ago. Would you mind?"

Dylan closed his eyes and placed a gentle kiss on Ali's lips. He ran his hand over his soft cheek and down his arm until they were holding hands. "Oh, my God, you're amazing Ali", he said whilst brushing his hair out of his man's face with his free hand.

Yes, in that moment of tenderness, Dylan had decided that Ali was definitely 'his man'. He was so different from George in every way possible. There was no rush, grapple, rough hands, groans, or feverish relief. This was just beautiful, calm and natural. Both men fell together on the bed and just kissed and hugged. Ali gazed at Dylan and said,

"Please don't leave. Stay tonight and let me wake up in your arms. I've never done that before with any-one."

I'd love to wake up holding you. But will you do me a massive favour, please?"

"What do you want, handsome?"

"I want you to feel comfortable with me. I guess you don't sleep wearing trousers or your prosthesis, do you? "

Tears dripped down Ali's face. But sometimes actions are better than words. He got up off the bed, grabbed his crutch, disappeared into the bathroom and returned ten minutes later wearing nothing more than a pair of crisp white boxer shorts. Ali could feel Dylan wrap himself around him, lean in and kiss him before they fell arm-in-arm into a deep sleep together.

# Chapter Six

The rancid rattle of the tube and plumes of car fumes welcomed the couple into central London. They wandered through Oxford Street, carefully avoiding the tourists who had a nasty habit of stopping dead with no warning. There had been many a time when Dylan had almost fallen onto some unsuspecting stranger. The men got a takeaway coffee and a three-cheese bap before heading into Soho Square Gardens. Only the best was good enough for them. They claimed their patch of grass in the sun opposite the gardener's hut and settled down for the afternoon. Dylan couldn't have been happier if he'd tried. Ali was his North, East, South and West rolled into one beautiful man. Once they were suitably refreshed, the lovers enjoyed their second favourite activity. They lay backwards and began to cloud gaze together.

"Look at that one there. It looks like a dog," Dylan said, pointing at the sky.

"Oh, god, you're right. I adore animals. When I was growing up in foster care, Alf and Rita had a German Shepherd named Shep. He was soft as a brush. I loved running my fingers in between his coat and lying with him on the hearth.

"When I think about it, Alf and Rita had a lot to put up with. I'm so grateful that they didn't give up on me. I roared like a lion and neither of them had a full night's sleep for years. They were the last chance saloon for me. I had already been moved from placement to placement and was heading for a children's home. But they are amazing people. I still see them now from time to time.

"There's always at least one child living with them when I go around. I don't know how they do it," Ali replied as he found Dylan's hand.

"But you had every right to be angry. You're the strongest person who I know. Losing your parents in a car crash is tragic. That's more than enough for any child to cope with. But also losing your leg in the same accident doesn't even bear thinking about. And yet, here you are. You're the kindest and most selfless person I've ever met."

"I didn't have a choice. I just had to get on with it as best I could. It was all down to Alf and Rita." Ali replied whilst watching the dog turn into the shape of a camel.

"I'm sorry, but I disagree. We all have a choice in this life to either be a victim or to use our experiences as a strength to help others. You're just amazing," Dylan stopped mid-sentence, thought for a split second and said, "Ali, I love you."

Ali looked at him directly in his eyes and stroked his lover's face. "I love you too. I do."

Dylan finally understood what love was all about. It was real, uncomplicated, tender, and unhurried. There were no grand gestures, sonnets, romantic music or university halls to contend with. A soggy cheese bap, an instant coffee and a grass-stained back was more than enough as long as Ali was by his side.

Dylan took the red stethoscope that had crossed around his neck, straightened his collar, and tried his best to dampen down his hair. Even before he got through the ward doors, he spotted a change. A burgundy notice board had mysteriously appeared to the left of the entrance. Someone had pinned all the usual phone numbers and visiting times in gold plastic letters. He gulped as he clocked the name of the consultant sitting proudly with the Sister. Like an extra in 'Stars In Their Eyes', he catapulted through the doors with a creak rather than the mist of dry ice. Instead of spotting a grinning Mathew Kelly, a group of milling junior doctors welcomed his entrance. But at least everyone on the television show knew that the acts were pretending to be someone else. Even the famous 'Tonight Mathew I'm going to be' line wouldn't save him here. Taking a deep breath, he checked his pocket watch, smiled at Grace, and started his routine. With a bit of luck, no one would notice his legs shaking under his doctor's coat.

A blonde-haired man sat bolt upright on the starched white sheets. He was wearing an oversized black silk dressing gown with golden piping. Heavy intravenous syringe drivers burdened a drip stand to the right of his bed, pumping a plethora of medication into him. A bag of liquid feed dripped slowly through a nasogastric tube and into the man's stomach. A spaghetti of elephant trunking and a large oxygen mask almost hid his withered face. On seeing Dylan, he smiled and tried to talk. But through his pursed lips, it was almost impossible to string a sentence together. Instead, he settled on a raspy 'Hello'. Dylan grabbed a chair and took hold of the young man's hand, being careful not to dislodge the infusions. An olive-skinned man sat opposite, huddled in a green bomber jacket and also holding his patient's other free hand.

Dylan smiled at them both. "I've got some good news, Craig. I've had a look at your latest chest x-ray and blood results. We're not out of the woods just yet, but we seem to be keeping this pneumonia at bay. I know it doesn't look like it at the moment, but there has been some slight improvement. We're heading in the right direction."

"Thank you, Dr Dylan," Craig said as he wheezed and gripped hold of his consultant's hand.

"Remember, I'm here for the both of you. Just ask our lovely Sister Grace or any of my team to contact me if you need anything." And with that, Dylan continued his ward round under the watchful eye of Grace. Moving her to the infectious diseases ward was the only thing he had insisted on. After all, if anyone was going to prop up a new consultant, then it was her.

---

Dylan fell through the rather stiff entrance door to their apartment and shouted down the hallway, "Hi Darling, I'm home."

Ali saw his man struggling to close the door and smirked. No amount of swearing or pushing was helping the cause. For a consultant supposedly at the top of his game, he really was making a meal out of this simple task. "Come here, let me help. There's a knack to it. Oh Lord, you seem so stressed. Let me give you a quick fingering before we go any further. No, I mean your neck!"

Dylan felt much better after inhaling his man's patchouli shampoo and Armani aftershave. Ali's firm thumbs instinctively began kneading his shoulders as they embraced. He then followed his man into the kitchen. As the stained glass door swung open, his tastebuds ached for the roast beef that was browning in the red alga. Out was the soulless chipboard carcasses and in was the traditional shaker-style cream kitchen, double Belfast sinks and butcher block countertops. The refit was worth every penny to see Ali happy. Dylan was a terrible cook but was content to sip red wine and watch from the safety of the kitchen island. And to be perfectly frank, as much as Ali loved him, too many cooks spoiled the broth. He may have called the shots at work, but Ali was well and truly in charge of the interior design. The entire house would have looked like a flat-pack nightmare otherwise. They spent many happy hours rummaging through antic stores and flea markets, looking for the perfect pieces to fill their home.

Dylan's glasses steamed up as the oven door flung open. Ali took out a tray of roast beef and seasonal vegetables and proudly plonked them on the island. He wiped the heat from his forehead and shouted over the sizzle, "Ta-da, only the best will do for my handsome new consultant. And goodness me, don't those glasses make you look hot? You should've bought a pair years ago."

"Thank you for going to all of this trouble for me, darling. It smells delicious. I'm a very lucky man. "

"It's the least I can do. I know you are more of a meat and two-veg man than fancy food. It must be your northern roots."

Now munching on a carrot, Dylan said, "Well, you won't believe it, but I think they even have running water up north these days. But seriously, thank you for making my night so special. I've had a pig of a day. There was a young couple on my ward round earlier. And just like us, you could tell that they were in love. None of this is getting any easier. I felt useless."

"But you're not useless Dylan. Never forget that." Ali leaned over the counter to give his man a gravy-flavoured kiss.

"Anyway, what's on the agenda for tomorrow? You've got me all to yourself," Dylan said, wiping the stickiness from his lips. "Shall we go to that antique warehouse again? I fancy a calved-four poster for our bedroom. There's enough floor space and the ceilings will take it. We could even get some of those voile drapes to hang from it. I'm sick of sleeping in our low bed. It's doing nothing for my back."

"Mmmm, let's just see what there is first, darling. You've not been reading 'Princess and the Pea' in the children's ward again, by any chance? "

# Chapter Seven

Maria sunk her head further into her soggy feather pillow. Why on earth had anyone thought that the pickings from a goose's arse could provide any comfort? She picked it up, wiped the make-up from her three-hundred-thread count peach pillowcase and slung it across her bedroom. Bullseye. She hit her target even with one eye shut. Clambering from her sweaty pit, she rested her head on the pink-padded headboard and watched the silver-framed picture topple from her dressing table. The glass smashed into a thousand fragments onto her thick tufted shag. But why should she care? No one would recognise her now in that grainy black-and-white photo. They'd lived the life of the Munsters rather than the Kennedys, anyway. But at least Lily and Herman actually loved each other. What did she have to show for it? One dead son, another one who hardly spoke to her, and a faggot of a husband. But even he'd left her now.

None of this would've happened if she hadn't married the lying bastard in the first place. But it was too late. How had she been so stupid? But George made her feel like a princess when they had first met. With Queen Victoria glaring at them, he'd been all over her like a rash when they were courting. A lot more than the price of bacon came up in between those feverish fumbles in fuchsia bushes. And she'd loved every minute of it. There was no way of knowing that he was as bent as a five-bob note. And when he sang 'Maria' to her, her heart missed a beat. The git had even sung the same song during his marriage proposal at his graduation from medical school. And she'd swallowed his bullshit hook, line, and sinker. Maria could hardly contain herself when she told Jane about the marriage proposal. But a lot of water had passed under the bridge since then. Jane had died and Dylan had mysteriously disappeared the same night of the graduation ball. He'd gone to London the very next day without so much as a goodbye. All he had to do was to swallow his pride, but he stormed off down south. As George had said, if Dylan had feelings for her, then he should've owned up in the first place. That would've been the decent thing to do. Perhaps they could have all remained friends. But now, she would never know.

Maria tasted the stringy sputum in her mouth, smacked her lips and reached for the bottle of bubbly that stood on the mahogany bedside table. Only the best would do for her. This wasn't her usual bottle of plonk that she picked up from the offy on the way home most nights. She'd been rotating the off licenses. It just wasn't cricket for such a prominent bank manager to be found clinking her way through life. Maria grabbed the Monet and gulped directly from the bottle. Well, it was only fitting to be celebrating. She belched, laughed and slurred a toast to George.

"Fuck off, you fucking arsehole. Even when you were found fucking around in those toilets, I stuck by you. And now I'm finally free. Good riddance, you fucking puff." And with that, she passed out once again, spilling the fizz all over the Cottage Blossom quilt.

Maria didn't get hangovers anymore. As the alarm buzzed in the new day, she felt the wet mess under her with the back of her hand and then sniffed it. That was a relief; it was just the champagne. It hadn't been the first time that she'd wet herself. That's what credit cards and bin bags were for anyway. It was just easier to scoop any soiled bedding up, drop them in the bin before anyone noticed, and buy some more on the way home. She was now on first-name terms with the ladies who worked behind the till in the homeware store. They thought Maria was an absolute saint to treat all of her friends and family to such luxury regularly. She rolled off the bed, half landed on her feet and farted. Without spewing this time, it was safe to slip into her moccasins. Well, that bloody frame had shattered everywhere and she couldn't be too careful.

The water felt good on her body. But that was the only thing that she liked about the shower cubicle. Leaning against the cold pink tiles, Maria shook her head at the rolls of fat that hung from her ageing body. As she lifted her sagging breasts to clean the sweat rashes, she tumbled onto the floor. Ouch. God, it was still sore under there despite the anti-fungal cream. Now crouching like a Sumo Wrestler, even the water didn't drown out her wails. This time, she hadn't hurt herself. This was something far worse. In that blubbery moment, Maria realised she had wasted her life on a dream that'd never belonged to her.

"Your Father and I have split up, darling. We're getting a divorce. I know that this will come as a shock to you, but we haven't been getting on for a very long time," Maria explained, while taking a sip out of a bone china mug that Christian reserved for her visits.

"I'm sorry to hear that, Mother," he said, glancing at Carla. "Both of you deserve to be happy. "

"Thank you for your understanding son, I don't doubt that this will be very upsetting for you both. Especially with a baby of your own on the way. I don't know where your father has gone, but I imagine he'll be in touch when he's good and ready."

Carla squeezed Christian's hand tighter. She sighed, and there and then, confronted her mother-in-law. She looked directly into her eyes and said, "Well, Mrs Taylor-"

"—You mean Mother, I've told you many times to call me that. Us girls need to stick together in this family."

"Well, then, *Mother*, let's stop kidding ourselves, shall we?" We already know that you've split up. George phoned us yesterday. He didn't say much other than that he's gone to live in London for now. Oh, and by the way, he said that the divorce is not your fault. Apparently, you want different things out of life and both deserve a crack at happiness.

"Christian has told me about his childhood, Maria. So, while we're at it, let's get it all out in the open. If we're going to move forward as a family, then you need to be honest with us. I don't need to know all the gory details. That belongs to George and yourself. But I refuse to bring up my child in a pack of lies. I won't let history repeat itself.

"And yes, while we're rubbing the slate clean, we know all about Jack, too. He was gay, wasn't he? And you turned your back on him, didn't you? Remember, it's a very small world. The family that he made for himself just happens to be part of our friendship group. My boss, Max, was very close to your son. He's still grieving for him now, although he won't admit it to anyone. Well, there you go. You had this coming."

Maria couldn't believe what she was hearing. "Oh my God, what have I done? All of this time you knew about Jack and everything and you never said a word!"

Carla continued, "Yes, I kept my gob shut to keep the peace, but now I've had enough of all the lies. Maria, mother or whatever the hell you want me to call you, there's a place for you in our lives. Sadly, my own mother died of cancer and will never get the chance to see her grandchild. But you must be honest with us.

"We don't expect you to be perfect. None of us are. Trust me on that one. But how do you expect us to trust you with our child if you can't be genuine with Christian and me?"

"You're right. I've been a complete and utter bitch. But I'll change. I'm not trying to defend or justify my hideous behaviour either, but there's a lot more to all of this than you will ever understand," Maria said.

"I don't doubt that. We all have regrets in life. I've made my fair share of mistakes over the years. But here's my line in the sand. No more lies, right? Do you understand?"

"Yes, no more lies, Carla. I get it, promise."

Christian cleared his throat and piped up, "Mother, Carla is right. You know that deep down. I've been struggling that both you and Dad lied to me about Jack. He was my brother, and I didn't even get the chance to say goodbye. But you're my mother and I love you, even after everything that you've said and done over the years."

"I'm not sure that I've earned your love, Christian, but I'll do everything to make it up to you. I haven't been much of a mother. But I promise, with all of my heart, to be a much better grandmother."

And at that precise moment, Maria realised what she was going to do with the rest of her life.

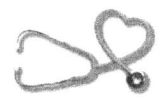

Maria trundled up with another bag of baby wear and opened the door to her apartment. Selling that Victorian pile was the best decision she'd made over the last eight months. And when a two-bedroom flat became available in a purpose-built swanky retirement complex within spitting distance of town, she jumped at it. But how on earth had she ever found the time to work in the first place? In between her yoga and flower arranging classes, becoming a 'lady that lunches', her endless shopping expeditions and sitting on her balcony just content watching the world go by with a cup of herbal tea, she didn't miss her job at the bank at all. She looked at her watch, sprang to her feet and flounced into town.

Carla waddled into the restaurant and found Maria already waiting at a table near the toilets. Thank goodness for that, at least. Baby Jack had a habit of sitting on her bladder. But it was all definitely worth it, and it wasn't long before her maternity leave started. To be honest, since Max had found out that she was pregnant, he'd wrapped her up in cotton wool at work anyway. Over the clatter of plates, Maria pulled a soft toy, a pack of blue baby grows and matching tiny booties from her handbag. "Just don't go mad with me darling, I couldn't resist these. They're so cute. Look how soft this teddy is."

"Thank you, Maria. I don't want to appear ungrateful, but this isn't your way of buying away your guilt, is it?"

"No, it's not. But I don't blame you for asking. I just want to be part of Jack Junior's life when he makes his appearance."

Changing the subject, Carla asked, "Have you heard from George?"

As casually as pouring another cup of peppermint tea, Maria said,

"Yes, the divorce is in progress. I've signed all the papers. Half of the house belongs to him, anyway. That's only fair. Funnily enough, we were talking on the phone only the other night.

"I think we could become good friends if we tried, you know. He sounds happy. We've done all the sorry stuff together and are moving on. I just wish we'd been brave enough to do this years ago. It would've saved such a lot of pain for everyone. I realise that now.

"He told me he has bought a lovely little flat in Putney with indirect views of the Thames, whatever that means. He's coming up when the baby is born. Did you know? "

"I did. Christian talks to him all the time these days. You're right, he seems much happier. I'm just glad that you've finally found some peace between you."

My staff had done us proud once again. The day room looked like a Disney fairy tale. Blue paper bunting in the shape of rabbits hung from the ceiling. Even the patients were roped into the preparation. They had painted a three-foot "It's A Boy" banner which was pinned along the cream wall. Carousel tables with blue and white gingham cloths displayed a buffet that was fit for royalty. A beautiful two-tier cake presided over trays of food. This work of art looked almost too good to eat. The larger white base layer had building blocks around it, spelling out the word baby in indigo icing. A taller powder blue layer sported a circle of white icing balloons around the edge. In crowning glory, a beautiful sugar-crafted teddy bear peered out at us. I had no idea that Poppy had such skills; it was so kind of her to make it for Carla.

As I walked down the ward to thank the staff for their gallant efforts, my eyes rested on one of our latest recruits, a healthcare assistant named Billy. I could see the *Oh shit* look in his eyes when he clocked me, beckoning him over with my finger. I'd heard on the jungle drums that he'd been like a rat up a drainpipe with all the young girls who worked at the hospital. But none of this washed with me. Shaking my head, I said,

"I'll see you in my office in five minutes. Don't be late."

He smirked, huffed and collapsed into a chair opposite my desk. Whilst blowing his golden locks off his face, he said, "What's wrong now, Max? You've got it in for me."

"How dare you, young man? Let me tell you, I've lost count of the times that I've had to talk to you. And for your information, I certainly don't have it in for you. I'm not like that. But you don't learn. We have a dress code for a reason.

"And whilst I love the John Bon Jovi vibe that you've got going on, there's a time and place for everything. Please tie your hair back for work. It's not rocket science. Everyone else seems to manage it. Now, I assume you'd prefer *me* to tell you rather than the senior staff who are coming to Carla's baby shower. I can't imagine Danni, Jan, Eunice, or Shirley being so patient with you, Billy!"

"I'm sorry boss, I'll tie it back."

"And make sure you keep it that way. Close the door behind you on your way out." Oh my god, this wasn't one of the finer moments of my reign, even if he'd got under my skin. I had to abdicate before I became Jane Body or Emily Dickson. My navy tunic top was choking me.

There was a flurry of activity coming down the stairs and toward the ward doors. I stumbled out of my office and slapped on a smile. Carla's send-off would be amazing, even if it was the death of me. A group of patients and staff were putting the finishing touches to the decorations as I arrived. My eyes rested on Billy, who was gently helping Ethel to scatter foiled confetti around the tables. Even this had shapes of baby rattles and teddy bears cut into the shiny blue foil. She looked at the smart blonde man who was guiding her good arm and said,

"Thank you, duck. If only I was sixty years younger, you wouldn't stand a chance. It's been a very long time since I've had such a stud muffin on my arm. You're making an old lady very happy."

"Now, don't get carried away. I don't want you to have another stroke because of me. Think of your blood pressure," Billy replied.

As I got closer to the frivolity, Ethel said, "Stand by your beds! Here comes the boss."

"I'm glad that Billy is keeping you entertained. They say that laughter's the best medicine." I winked and continued, "he's a good lad, but will you keep an eye on him for me please Ethel? It's a case of give him an inch and he'll take a yard."

"Oh my dear life, I'd like to see that, Max. It'd certainly make an old lady very happy. What a way to go!"

"Right, I'd better see if I have a bottle of bromide in the medicines cupboard before you do yourself a mischief! Thank you Billy. You're doing a great job here. Keep up the good work. You look very smart by the way, with those locks tied back."

There was a flurry of hushed silence as Poppy led Carla into the dayroom. She'd no idea of our dastardly plans, let alone that we were hiding there in the dark. I thought she was going to give birth right there on the spot when we turned on the lights and shouted 'Surprise!' But thankfully, the only waters to break were tears running down her face. Seeing the genuine respect and love she received from everyone at the Eastfield was priceless. She had truly settled in. I noticed that Doctor Lock had made the effort to attend as I scanned the crowd. Danni and her were as thick as thieves in the corner of the room.

I did the rounds, making polite conversation with everyone. But Carla and Christian were the actual stars of the show. It was lovely watching them holding hands whilst slowly circulating the room, taking time to speak to all the patients and staff alike. There were no airs or graces with this beautiful young couple. My mind drifted back to the first time I saw Enrolled Nurse Carla Jones sitting in that grotty accident and emergency nicotine den of a staff room. And now look at her, smoke-free, on the cusp of motherhood and with one of the kindest men that I'd ever met. Oh my god, I was having one of those 'netted orange bag' moments again. Well, if it was good enough for Arnold, then it was good enough for me. I half expected Harvey Fierstein to waltz in and sing 'Love for Sale'. Now that would've been a sight for sore eyes.

Over the top of Dolly's 'Jolene', laughter rang from the buffet tables. *Your beauty is beyond compare with flaming locks of auburn hair.* At any minute, Shirley and Eunice were going to aspirate and collapse on a plate of cheese and pickles. *With ivory skin and eyes of emerald green, your smile is like a breath of spring.* Wayne had them eating out of his hand. Now and again they looked over at me, sniggered, waved or both. *Your voice is soft as summer rain.* I'd no idea what they were talking about, but wasn't daft enough to go over and find out. Some things are better left unknown. *I cannot compete with you Jolene.* Jan sidled up to me, brandishing a plate of cold cuts and coleslaw. She looked even more like a young Nigella Lawson in her red fitted dress and matching lipstick. While chewing on a celery stick, she said,

"Max, I hate to steal you away from the party, but can I have a quick word with you? Don't worry though, you're not in trouble."

"Of course Jan, no problem. Shall we go to my office? I can't hear you properly here." What an earth did she want?

"Right Max. You're doing a good job down here, but I hear you're unhappy. Please don't worry, I understand."

I tried to stop my left leg from shaking with my hand. "I don't want to appear ungrateful, but I miss being at the bedside. Can I just ask if a certain parrot-wearing friend of mine squawked in your ear about this?"

"That's for me to know and for you to find out, Max. But I have news for you. We're currently working hand in hand with the university to model our nursing workforce. We're investing now to reap the benefits in the future. There are plans to train a cohort of advanced nurse practitioners. The business case has been approved at board by the directors.

"As you're aware, this involves completing a master's degree in advanced clinical practice. Our advanced nurse practitioner workforce will possess diagnostic authority and be trusted to assess, manage, prescribe medication, and provide care for patients with complex clinical issues. If I've got my facts right, then this is right up your street, isn't it?"

"Yes, that's where my heart is, Jan. I'd love to do that."

"Then why don't you apply and see what happens? You've our full support. If you're successful in getting on the course, then we'll release you from your current job to complete the study days. And more to the point, we've a pot of money available to draw down from region. It won't cost you a single penny.

"By that time, Carla will be back from her maternity leave. I know she'll step up when you aren't here. And who knows, a job may come up as an Advanced Nurse Practitioner whilst you're training."

"I'm speechless, thank you." I wanted to kiss her, but that would've been so inappropriate.

"Well, don't thank me yet. You haven't got on the course. And to be honest, it wasn't all entirely my idea. There've been a few people whispering in my ear. And don't ask me who they were. Right, let's get back to the baby shower before we're missed. I've got my eyes on a slice of that gorgeous-looking cake."

# Chapter Eight

George stood at the bus stop on the high street and idly admired the florist's selection of blooms behind him as he waited. The sunflowers caught his attention. They'd look lovely on the windowsill of his flat because they always looked like they were smiling. He'd put his roots down and purchased his home in a new development on the banks of the Thames. If you leaned out of the window, it was just possible to see the river in all its glory. Many times, he was content to mindlessly wander up the banks, taking in the views and stopping for a cappuccino whenever the mood struck him. He'd worked hard all of his life and now it was his time to do whatever he wanted whenever he felt like doing it. The number seventy-three screeched and jolted him back from his daydream. He got on, flashed his season ticket and headed to his favourite seat behind the driver. The bus rattled through the High Street, over Putney Bridge and through Fulham Palace Road. George never got sick of this view. He even got a quick glimpse of the football ground this time around. But instead of just getting off the bus and waiting for another one on the other side of the road to take him home again, today was different. He'd finally plucked up the courage to go into the hospital, albeit to the canteen only. But this was a miracle in itself. He swished through the hospital's automatic doors and recognised the smell of sanitised order. But none of this belonged to him anymore, thank god. His heart pounded over the top of the hustle and bustle of the busy concourse. Luckily, some kind soul had conveniently placed a row of plastic moulded chairs near the entrance doors. He sat and contemplated his future. Feeling a little calmer, he wiped the beads of sweat from his forehead with his hanky and carried on a little further.

He tailed a gaggle of London nurses towards the smell of the restaurant. From what he could gather, they were chatting about a battle axe of a sister who had chewed up some young nurse. Some things never changed. The restaurant was alive with hungry staff queuing by a large hot counter, waiting to get their curly fries and fish, soup of the day or a grilled toastie. All of which turned his stomach at the very thought. He grabbed a bottle of water from a cooler, paid at the fast track till and slowly headed over to the corner of the restaurant to get a bird's-eye view of the door. An uncomfortable metal chair grated on his back whilst he sipped and waited. Every time the door swung open, his heart missed a beat. But that was probably just his Atrial Fibrillation giving him jip.

A tower of dirty food trays provided just enough camouflage between George, the open door, and hopefully a glimpse of Dylan. They hadn't exactly parted on the best of terms in that piss-stained cubicle all of those years ago. He regretted with every silver hair on his head that he hadn't stood by the love of his life. Clattering back to reality, he squinted through the half-eaten food mounting on the trays. After an hour of waiting, he treated himself to another bottle of overpriced water. With a full bladder, he wandered into a green and white-painted public toilet. A plastic-coated wall had three separate urinals attached to it. Directly behind the urinals were a row of four cubicles. For reasons best known to the hospital planners, each door had been plastic coated in a different colour. The stench of toilet blocks hit the back of his throat, but at least the porcelain looked clean.

He disappeared behind red door number three, grappled with the stiff lock, and contemplated his fate. It was a ludicrous plan in the first place. Dylan was a busy man and probably ate his lunch at his desk whilst trying to do another thousand things. It wasn't all that long ago that he'd done the same. George opened the cubicle, rinsed his hands and then took it out on the poor paper towel dispenser that was refusing to play ball. He heard the echo of the restaurant greet him and then fade away. A man was awkwardly trying to pull the door open while George was pushing it in the other direction.

The man stumbled, grabbed onto the handle, and said,

"Oh, sorry, I didn't see you there. George, is that you? What are you doing here? Jesus Christ!"

"Hi, Dylan. Yes, it's me."

"Wait for me, George, will you? I'll be out in a minute. This isn't the time or place for a conversation."

George stood outside the toilets, feeling dazed whilst waiting for Dylan. He'd yearned for this moment, but now that it was happening, it was overwhelming. Dylan emerged from behind the door, dressed in a crisp white doctor's coat. As he moved, it flayed open, revealing a burgundy waistcoat, navy plaid tie, and blue slacks. His pockets held a red stethoscope and a medication formulary. His silver-rimmed glasses darkened in the sunlight. His short salt-and-pepper hair only added to his handsomeness.

"Are you OK George? Just sit for a minute before you fall over, will you? You look as white as my coat."

"I'm OK. I wasn't expecting to see you today, that's all." And that bit was true. He wasn't *expecting* to see the love of his life today, no matter how much he'd secretly prayed that it would happen.

Dylan looked at his watch, frowned, and shuffled from foot to foot. "Right, I was due in clinic ten minutes ago. I really must dash. It was good to see you, George. Give my regards to Maria, will you?"

George didn't want it to end like this. He panicked over the words that tumbled out of his dry lips, "Dylan, please, don't go, I'm begging you. Maria and I are divorcing. If I never get to speak to you ever again, then please know that I am sorry for everything that I have done. Please let me explain."

"I'm not sure that you need to. You owe me nothing. That's ancient history. But thank you for the apology. Now I need to go." And with that, Dylan spun on his black heal and disappeared.

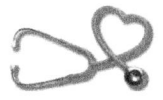

George was a spare prick in a brothel. A constant loop of blur vibrated through what was left of his nerves. Where was Elaine Paige when he needed her? Young handsome men lined the bar, gyrating to the beat, competing to be top cock. If they weren't careful, at least half of them would catch double pneumonia. This certainly wasn't the weather to be strutting around in next to nothing. This was the reason why he avoided coming up West. But needs must when the Devil drives. He wasn't going to miss the opportunity to see Harry again; even if he did feel inadequate against the backdrop of this sweaty testosterone. Harry waltzed into the pub, tipped his baseball hat at the bar staff and found George sitting alone at a table. Had someone not told him that tweed had gone out of fashion three decades ago?

"Come on, Grandad, I can tell how much you are loving it here. Let's go somewhere a little quieter, shall we?" Harry said whilst hugging George. "How about the theatre bar around the corner? I know you camp old queens love all of that."

George laughed, mimed a knife sticking through his chest, and hugged him. "Less of the old, will you? But yes, you're right. It makes me feel like a dirty old man here. My rain mack certainly doesn't have any buttons missing, let me tell you."

Once soothed by a show tune or maybe six, and a couple of drinks, George told his tale of woe to his unlikely friend. Harry wrote his name in the pile of his red velvet chair repeatedly as his friend vented his spleen. There was something about this young man George liked; he was kind, funny, thoughtful and had a good ear. Over the last few months, he had become quite taken with him when he was in town. But now, instead of listening to the behind-the-scene antics of 'Phantom', George was reliving the gory details of his own drama.

"Please! Have you learned nothing from me? Well, it's like this Grandad; you've two choices. You can either go back to your flat and spend the rest of your life feeling sorry for yourself or you can go to the hospital and make him listen to you," Harry said whilst chasing an ice-cube around the bottom of his tumbler.

"But it's not as easy as that, son. He made it crystal clear that our love boat sailed a long time ago."

Harry started casting a spell from an imaginary wand. "But this isn't the bloody Titanic, is it? Now you listen to me Dorothy, click your ruby slippers and get back to that hospital tomorrow. But this time, don't take 'No' for an answer. If you love him as much as you say, then he's worth the fight."

And that's exactly what George did. This time, Dylan wasn't getting away. He walked into the outpatient department, gave the nurse some flannel about being a visiting oncologist, found his office, and stormed in before anyone could stop him. He shouted over at Dylan,

"You'll listen to me if it's the last thing that I do!"

"OK, you win, but I can't talk now. Meet me later on. There's a pub across from the hospital. It's called Gatsby's Bar. Be there at six."

Overfilled ashtrays oozed toxic gunge over peeling black picnic tables. And the inside of the boozer was no better either. Why had Dylan chosen this dump? No, he wouldn't stand him up and leave him here, would he? Well, revenge is best served on a cold platter. George stuck to the floor as he made his way through the debris of wonky tables and ripped black leather chairs. He stood at the bar, not daring to put his hands down on the scratched dark wooden surface for fear of contracting some deadly disease. People had engraved names and the odd vulgar comment on the bar top. Someone at some point must have thought it was amusing to penknife 'Johnny sucks cocks' and' Sharron is a slut'. Well, at least they could spell. A chubby man, with dirty black hair and wearing the remains of his lunch down his green tee shirt, eventually tore himself away from the TV at the end of the bar for long enough to serve him. His breath stunk of fags and fried chicken. With the charm of a fresh corpse, he half looked at George and said,

"What do you want?"

George settled on a bottled coke as at least that hadn't been through the beer pumps, declined a glass and retreated to a booth by the door. The leather seating looked more like the Turin shroud than a place to relax, gather his thoughts, and plot his next move. Dylan appeared twenty minutes later from behind the smudged door and sat opposite George on the lumpy upholstery. With the pleasantries over, Dylan said,

"I haven't got long, so get to the point."

"I wasn't sure if you would turn up, but now that you're here, I want to be completely honest. I'm truly sorry for everything. There's not a day that has gone by when I haven't deeply regretted hurting you, choosing Maria, and lying to you. My life has been just one big mistake."

And then Dylan realised he was angry all over again with the creature who was sitting in front of him trying to get salvation in this filthy confessional box. The pain hadn't gone away. And how dare he walk back into his life and expect forgiveness? It didn't work like that. He'd made his bed and happily lay in it with Maria. And now, the bastard dared to say that he had come to his senses. Just who the hell did he think he was? "What happens if sorry is just not good enough?"

"Yes, you're right. It seems lame now, doesn't it? But please just give me a chance to explain everything. At least then you can say goodbye to me, knowing all the facts."

"But why should I care about you? You didn't give a flying fuck about me that night in the toilet cubicle, did you? I'd no choice but to leave. You humiliated me for the last time."

"But I've never stopped loving you."

"Bravo, bravo. How dare you walk in here with your crap and expect me to believe you," Dylan said.

George tried to hold back the tears by staring at a particularly suspect stain under their sticky table. "But, it's true Dylan, I love you and I always have. I've got no excuse for my actions."

Seeing these flickers of remorse defused Dylan's anger for now, at least. As they chatted, he slowly melted. He'd no idea about George's two sons, let alone that the younger one had died. Dylan didn't know that Jane was dead either. He'd been true to his word and really had said goodbye to everyone. But it turned out that the conversation wasn't all about George that evening after all.

"George, your timing couldn't have been any worse if you'd tried. But I shouldn't have shouted at you. I'm sorry too. It's been less than a year since I lost the love of my life to cancer. I'm all over the place. It started in his brain and by the time it was all over, it was easier to say where it hadn't metastasised. But you'll know all about that in your line of work. It's like preaching to the converted. I loved my Ali. Please understand."

"Yes, I understand. But it's completely different being on the other side of it, isn't it?"

"Yes, it certainly is. But you'll sadly know about that too, won't you? I'm so sorry that your lad's life was cut short. I'm sure you and Maria were devastated. Such a terrible thing to happen."

George's face dropped. He thought for a second and hung his head. "No more lies. I owe you that. No, Dylan, I was a terrible father."

Dylan blinked, adjusted his glasses and took a swig from his bottle. "Thank you for being honest with me. You didn't need to tell me that."

"You see, the thing is, I've got nothing to lose, have I? Tell me about Ali. A problem shared and all of that.

Swish-thud-swish-thud-swish-thud played over and over again. Dylan tried to calm his mind to the rhythm of this hypnotic beat. But it was no good. It was too easy to be jolted out of the zone by some unexpected distraction. He looked down and realised that he was picking at his fingers. Ali would go mad when he next saw his hands. Dylan had almost bitten his nails down to the bed and even started on the skin around his fingertips this time. He smiled and thought about his lover playfully scolding him every time that he had caught him chewing. Ali couldn't do that now. Despite lying in a hospital bed with a plastic tube sticking out of his mouth, he still looked beautiful. But as hard as he tried, Dylan just couldn't take his doctor's head off as he sat at the bedside. But he knew Ali was in expert hands. The team of doctors was seriously top-notch. If these neurosurgeons couldn't remove Ali's brain tumour safely, then no one could.

Dylan's tear-stained vision blurred the line between his heart and head. And it killed him. He sat fidgeting in his swivel chair behind his desk, talking to Tammy. But as per usual she never answered back. It was Ali who had named her in the first place. Dylan smiled and remembered his lover howling with laughter. On entering the wooden panelled room for the first time, Ali looked around and put one hand on his hip. "It's all a little butch in here, Dylan, even for you. This wooden desk looks more like the top of a coffin. It's sending shivers up and down my spine. We need to sprinkle a little glitter into here."

"I know, you're right. But beggars can't be choosers."

Ali's eyes scoured the room before landing on a dusty old medical skeleton. He curtseyed and looked into its eye sockets. "Well, it's a real pleasure to meet you, Miss Wynette. What brings you to this part of the world? Whilst you are here, I wonder if you could do me the honour of standing by my man. He gets a little stressed sometimes. It must be a northerner thing. The last thing we need is a D.I.V.O.R.C.E. Just cast your southern charm over him, will you?"

"Come here and kiss me. The only stress I have in my life is you constantly taking the Mickey out of me. But what is it about Tammy Wynette and gay men? We're like a moth to the flame when it comes to her."

"Oh, you're so stupid. Miss Wynette has had a tragic life, but has still harnessed her inner strength to shine. Do you get it now? If I didn't know what you are like in between the sheets, I would swear that you're straight sometimes."

For a moment, Dylan's finger hovered over the clunky 'enter' key. But it was a sackable offence to access the pathology system for personal use. And he *had* made that Hippocratic oath. But on the other hand, he wanted to know. Pre-armed was pre-warned. Tammy's advice sang in his head, *There are so many ways to love a man and so many ways to understand.* Would pressing the enter key make a difference in the end? *But there are so many ways to lose a man. So quickly he can slip through your hand.* Shuddering into a decision, he switched off the computer and sobbed. What were a couple of more days to wait for the histology results? It wouldn't change anything. *One little thing goes wrong, then all at once he's gone.* Even his doctor's coat couldn't shield them both. The weight was dropping off Ali at a rate of knots. *I'd no way to hold him like I planned. It takes more than just one way to love a man.* Dylan dried his eyes, slapped on his smile and left Tammy standing in the corner of his office.

The results were in and it wasn't good. Ali decided to focus on quality rather than quantity of life. In his mind, there was no point in prolonging the inevitable with a few rounds of palliative radiotherapy or chemotherapy. Whilst he was well, he wanted to enjoy each day until putting it bluntly, he couldn't. As the couple walked out of the Oncologist's office, Ali said,

"Let's put it this way, it's a good job that I have read all of Tolkien's Middle Earth series already. Not that I could now anyway, even if I wanted to. I can't concentrate on anything more taxing than the Good Housekeeping magazine. And even that makes me feel sick."

"How can you joke about this?"

"What else can I do? This thing's won."

And sadly, it had. The hospice at home service was amazing. In the end, everyone rallied around to help the couple. Grace stayed with them in between her shifts. She knew the couple needed her skills in different ways. It was much easier to jump into action and provide the practical nursing care that Ali needed than to soothe Dylan's distress. It was heartbreaking to watch him privately crumbling whilst publicly trying to keep it together in front of Ali. Even Alf and Rita came over and sat with them. But in the end, it was just the two of them. Dylan spooned his lover for the last time until the only noise in the room was the whirr of the syringe driver, which still pumped medication into Ali's lifeless body. But Dylan wasn't ready to let go just yet. He whispered into his man's cooling ear. "I love you so much. I know you have to go, but one day we'll be together again. I love you with all of my soul."

When he was good and ready, he released his embrace and signalled to Grace, Rita and Alf to join the couple on their four-poster. Alf cleared his throat, stroked Ali's clammy forehead and spluttered, "Goodbye, my son. Sleep well, my angel," before leaving with his wife.

Grace had other ideas. Leaning over the couple, she looked at Dylan and said, "Shall I give Ali a little wash, my precious? You can help me if you want to."

"That'd be lovely, Grace. He wouldn't want to look like a mess. And yes, let me help, please."

"Ok, my precious, but if it all gets too much, then let Gracie take over."

But it wasn't too much. This last act of love was the very least he could do for the man who had already given his entire heart to him.

George looked at the man sitting opposite him and wanted to cry. Although he was ashamed of the thoughts going through his head, he was jealous of Ali. How could he compete with a ghost? That would serve him right for asking about him. He cleared his throat and took another sip of the toxic substance from his bottle. "I'm so sorry for your loss. It's terrible when we lose some-one we love. I don't want to be insensitive, but is there any chance that we can be friends? Now that I've retired and have moved down here, I find myself very short of them. I'm just over the water in Putney these days. If it's too much, I understand. "

Dylan frowned. "You mean that you're not going back up north then? I didn't realise that you'd moved down here lock, stock and barrel."

"Yes. I'm here to make a new start. For the first time in years, I feel free. I know all the best coffee shops, but it gets so lonely going on my own."

"Right, I have to go. Unlike some of us, I still have to work. I've an early ward round in the morning. Goodnight. But in answer to your question, I'd love to come over the bridge and meet you for a coffee from time to time. Ali taught me that life is too short for regrets. And isn't it convenient that you live so near?"

# Chapter Nine

With the precision of a sniper, he straightened the pink satin bed cover, swung shut the battered wardrobe door and just about got out in time. Phew, that was a close one. His mother's shrill voice floated upstairs towards him. "Darling, we're back from the freezer centre. We've got a real treat for tea. Dad and I have bought some of those stuffed garlic chicken breasts that you have been hinting at. Oui, Oui Monsieur." Hearing the voice getting a little closer, Billy darted across the landing, catapulted onto his bed and just about grabbed his comic before his mother put her head around the door. "Hello, darling, did you hear me? We'll dine like the Queen tonight."

"Mum, that'd be lovely, thank you. Can we have crinkle-cut chips too, or is that pushing it?"

She put her hands on her hips, glared and waved her finger at him. "Have you been in our bedroom again? I've told you that you're not allowed in there. You've better not broken anything. I'm getting a bloody lock fitted to keep you out, young man. That'll teach you," and then she screamed to her husband, who was dutifully unloading their treasures into their new chest freezer, "Lenard, will you come upstairs this minute? He's been at it again. I'm sick of talking to him. And after everything that we do for him."

Billy heard his father's heavy footsteps bang upstairs as his mother huffed into their bedroom across the landing. Muffled shouting echoed from behind their walls. His parents stomped across the foam back, almost shaking the stair rails off their runner. Bang. The flimsy door nearly fell off its hinges. Mum shook the life out of a black and silver dress. As she waved it, the sequins caught the light and glittered on Billy's artexed ceiling. She almost crushed the wire coat hanger with her bony hand. "Billy, look what you've done. You've broken the zip. This is my best dress. How could you? And even if I can get it repaired, I doubt that the lipstick and mascara will ever come out. It's dry-clean only. You've ruined it. What am I going to wear to your father's work do next week? Enough is enough. Why do you keep doing this? Boys don't wear dresses, it's not right. I've told you to keep out of my things."

"Yes, Mum, I'm sorry. I won't do it again," he said as the evidence ran down his cheek. But that's all he could get out. There was no point arguing with her or even trying to explain. It'd only make her worse. His parents left the room talking about putting away the Tutti Frutti before it turned into a milkshake. To be honest, he didn't even like wearing that Joan Collins knockoff. That cocktail dress certainly wasn't for a young girl about town. It felt more like a Brillo pad against his soft legs as he squeezed himself into it. Next time he'd remember to apply his make-up first, though.

Billy felt like Eve in the Garden of Eden as the bathroom door opened. But instead of an apple, something far greater than the usual crocheted Dolly loo roll cover tempted him. There'd been many a time he'd faked constipation to play with her. But even Dolly couldn't compete with the beauty hanging over the bathtub. And who would have thought that his best friend's mother had such good taste? Colin had certainly kept that one quiet. Before he knew what he was doing, the red velvet was hugging his hips. He flicked his neck-length blonde locks back, moved from side to side, and admired himself in the mirror. Then he stopped, grabbed hold of an airbrush and sang, *Pappa I know you're going to be upset because I was always your little girl. But you should know by now that I'm not a baby.* Well, if it was good enough for his idol Madonna, then it was certainly good enough for him.

Before he could say as much as 'material girl', Colin barged in. He stared at his friend, who was trying to clamber out of his mother's dress with the elegance of a drunken penguin. "Billy, quick, let me help you. I've just heard my mum's car coming up the drive. She'll kill me if she catches you."

Billy stepped out of the dress and returned it to the hanger just as the key turned in the door. He looked at his friend and said, "Thanks. You won't tell anyone, will you?"

"Don't be silly, Billy," he smiled, "friends are friends, right? I know you aren't really into football, but let's have a kick about with the other boys on the green before anyone suspects anything."

Colin's kindness made each day a little more bearable. Kids are cruel and there were only so many times that he could be called 'Billy No Mates' or even worse, before he believed it.

With the taste of salmon paste still on his breath, Billy went to his safe place for the rest of his dinner break. But this time he remembered to rinse his hands before falling foul to Miss Tatton again. Nobody wanted to read a library book coated in his cheesy puff fingerprints, no matter how enthralling the story might be. As he entered the school library, she sat in her green twin piece and tight grey bun. On spotting him, the librarian raised her eyebrows and then inspected his hands. Once Mrs Tatton was satisfied that his hands were clean, she allowed him to take his usual spot in the corner of the reading nook. In no time, he became engrossed in a mythical world where anyone could be anything.

He had a stash of birthday cash burning in his pocket. Well, you're only seventeen once. It was a total surprise that he got to town in the first place, as the driver could hardly see through the nicotine-stained windows and persistent drizzle. This grimy paradise, filled with cafes, chip wrappers, and the bus station's men's toilets, was his spiritual home. But today, for a change, he had more than his dinner money to squander. Billy wasn't sure if it was the escalator or his knees that juddered the most as he made his way up to the second floor. Surely, the department store was big enough for him to go undetected? After all, no one had noticed that the same canned music had tinkled away in the background for at least three years. Half of him wanted to turn around and catch the escalator back down immediately. But he'd been on this hamster wheel for far too long. He plucked up the courage, jumped into the ladies' department and landed facing an end gondola of underwear. His face burned as he scuttled past nylon-smelling bra and knickers sets. It was difficult trying to look casual, with a face full of frills in his eyeline. Fantastic. Mission accomplished. Taking a sideways look, he grabbed the white tennis skirt and matching top off the display and joined the queue to pay, hoping that no one would ask him questions. And to his relief, the ladies who stood behind the till seemed far more interested in gossiping about some cow of a line manager than noticing that a young man was purchasing them. Well, it was probably for his sister, anyway. After safely shoving his treasure into the department store's plastic bag, he breathed. The other girls at school got to wear summer PE uniforms, so why on earth couldn't he? Finally, he had something of his own that belonged to him. And better still, it fit like a glove. He lay on his bed and imagined playing tennis with the other girls in the sixth form in the summer heat without those horrible shorts weighing him down. He was a girl. So why was he made to wear boys' clothes? It just wasn't fair. In a world where trans wasn't even a word, how could he tell anyone?

Billy came home from college and tore his bedroom apart. Where was it? Who had stolen his tennis skirt and top from under his bed? Why? Although Dad said nothing, Billy knew it was him. The bastard. Still shaking in silence, he joined his parents in the lounge. It was just easier to smile and play happy families, no matter how much it was crucifying him. The opening theme music of Carla Lane's '*Butterflies*' rang his arrival in the room. *Love is like a butterfly, as rare and gentle as a sigh.* What was going on? *The multicoloured moods of love are like its satin wings.* As bold as brass, Wendy Craig's shaggy-haired TV son strutted onto the screen wearing a T-shirt with 'I am a Transvestite' slapped across the chest. But nobody said anything. Instead, Mum got up from her throne and switched the TV channel over, grumbling about having to pay to watch rubbish. But the seed was planted.

The very next day, with the bit between his teeth, Billy found his way to church. He crept through the glass doors, flashed his library card and headed down the central aisle, desperately trying to find the answer to his prayers. And here, in these dusty archives, the penny finally dropped. He wasn't alone. His eyes scoured every syllable of April Ashley's *'Odyssey'* from cover to cover. He wept as he read of April's life as starting out as a boy in Liverpool, and later becoming famous as Britain's most glamorous person to have a sex change. It took courage and determination to make this transformation to become her true self. Billy lay on his bed that night, reliving every word. If April Ashley could get through life, then there was hope for him. With a spring in his step, he returned to the library the next day, sat down and read Jan Morris' *'Conundrum'*. The book spellbound him from start to finish. Jan Morris, born James, knew she was a female trapped in a man's body from the age of three. Billy sat in awe as he read Jan's deeply personal memoir of someone who ultimately fought for her right to be happy as herself and carry on living life on her terms. Finally, there was a glimmer of something.

The smell of stale beer and sweat clung to the eiderdown like sin. He smacked his crusty lips together, opened one eye, and groaned. What the hell had happened last night and, more to the point, who was this naked woman lying in the bed next to him? He threw his head back on the pillow and tried to remember the previous night while a thousand drills played *'Bat Out of Hell'*. He hadn't, surely not? Fuck. The last thing he remembered was standing at the bar listening to rock music in his black jeans and Iron Maiden T-shirt. How had he ended up in bed with a stranger who looked like she'd been dug up? The mystery woman opened her eyes, stared at the alarm clock and said in a Jordie accent,

"Good morning, Pet. Look, I've got to go. My husband will be back in after his night shift soon. But thanks for the bed and-"

"- And what? I can't remember anything," Billy asked.

"Oh, I see. If I'm perfectly honest, you were too drunk for anything, Pet. But if you want to try again, I'll be in the bar later on, after nine-thirty though," she said whilst gathering her clothes and scuttling off into the Newcastle morning.

It was impossible to comprehend quantum physics whilst the lecture theatre was spinning. And every time it stopped, his thoughts landed on that woman lying spread eagle and butt naked on his bed. The lecturer's voice just droned in the background as he picked the woman's hair off his T-shirt. Once the torment was over, he slung a heavy bag over his shoulder and returned to his pigeonhole in the halls of residence. The taste of her 'Poison' perfume and sweat still hung in the air. But any attempt to expel the sin could wait. Billy grappled with the stiff window until a cool breeze blew through the room, poured himself a pint of lukewarm water, and collapsed onto the bed. A blind rattled to fanfare his return from unconsciousness. In that space between sleep and awake, strange things were happening. Surely this wasn't Groundhog Day, was it? He shivered, farted, and willed himself back into the room. That was a close one. Just because his bed still smelt of her, didn't mean the woman was still there.

While swilling down a sausage roll and a spicy pot noodle with flat coke, he contemplated his next move. Maybe she could purge him clean. Whether he liked her or not, she was still the first woman who'd shown any interest in him. Yes, that was it. She was a pretty safe bet. After all, *she was singing proud* whilst her husband was on the night shift. But what should he wear? Once showered, washed and his breath smelling less like a dog's butt, he stood pondering at the fitted wardrobe door. In his heart, he knew what he wanted to wear, but decided on his leather trousers, a white laced shirt and a pair of black Dock Martin boots. It was always fashion before food. He'd been like a kid in a sweet shop in those swanky department stores. Dressing for two had nearly wiped out his student grant already. But it was a price worth paying. The smoothness of the leather felt so comforting against his slender legs. Before slipping into his hollow laced shirt, he stretched in front of the greasy mirror to examine Frankenstein's monster. Instead of a suture, he grabbed a blow dryer until those blonde locks danced around his face. There, his creature was complete.

Bohemian Rapsody vibrated through his torso as he leaned against the window to the 'Fallen Angel'. Originally called 'The Sphere' in the swinging sixties, because of the semi-circular frontage, this boozer now hosted the local rock gods and goddesses. The pub was painted head to foot in black, except for a purple stage. This hosted both local and visiting bands every weekend. Billy headed up the steps and into the pub. Once past the large wood barrels which served as tables, he landed at the glossy bar. A slightly built woman, with ginger combed hair and wearing more make-up than a drag queen's doppelgänger, tittered over. She raised her heavily studded eyebrows, which was a feat in itself, chuckled and said,

"Hi Billy, I see you are back for more tonight, then. Oh my goodness, Pet, you did us proud last night on that Karaoke machine. When you sang 'Livin' on a Prayer', it was just like having Jon Bon Jovi here. Let me get you a pint. This one's on the house."

"The truth is Jackie, I can't remember any of it," Billy replied, almost swallowing his teeth. "Did I get up on the stage?"

"Get up there, Pet, I couldn't keep you off it. Not that anyone minded with a voice like that and the body to go with it too. Don't you remember taking your shirt off and throwing it in the crowd?" Jackie said whilst knocking the head off a pint of lager.

"No, I don't remember anything. That's the thing."

"Don't you remember grabbing Chloe from the audience and slow dancing with her on the stage? I'm surprised that you went for her though, but then again, you had your beer goggles on. She's been around the block a bit. There were a lot of girls dying to get up there with you."

"Oh shit, I'm meeting her here later. At least I know her name now," he replied whilst gulping half a pint back.

Billy waited at the bar, wondering what on earth to do. Whilst this woman may be the key to unlocking his latent masculinity, he certainly didn't want to get into any more bother. But by the time he had batted off a few requests from the drinkers for an encore, and drunk another pint, Chloe had arrived in all of her star-spangled Lycra glory. He was sure that it must have been fashionable somewhere to wear a skin-tight black jumpsuit, a lace netted blouse, three-inch stilettos with chains attached to each heel and perhaps the biggest matching perm he'd seen this side of the eighties. As she got closer, he could smell her heavy perfume, which, despite his best efforts, still lingered like death in his room. What had he done? As he attempted to air kiss her, she grabbed him by the buttocks until he was face to face with the gap in her teeth and pressed up against her undulating ripples. Looking around the bar, she shouted over the top of Meatloaf,

"Well, lover boy. We're way past all the formalities by now. Come here and give us a snog."

Billy froze on the spot, but luckily Jackie lunged over the bar to divert his date. "Hello, Chloe, is it the usual, Pet?"

Chloe smiled and loosened her grip a little. "Oh, yes, please and get this lovely young man here another drink while you are at it."

The more Billy chatted with Chloe, the more he liked her. She was upfront and honest and didn't try to be anything that she wasn't. Whilst she was best friends with her husband, it would always be tumbleweed in the bedroom department. But she knew this before marrying her Mickey. At least he offered her a roof over her head, kindness and companionship. All the things that weren't available in her first marriage. They were more like brother and sister than man and wife. Mickey worked four nights a week at a local casino as a dealer on the poker table. Male players who sat at his table offered such a handsome man with Greek Heritage far more than casino chips in tips. And should the mood take him, Mickey was happy to oblige. This left Chloe free to wander the rock scene, looking for someone to play with her own slot machine. And when Billy dragged her up onto the stage the previous night, she'd hit the jackpot.

Before he realised what he was doing, Billy was in the back of a cab and on the way to Chloe and Mickey's three bedroom semi-detached. From the outside, it looked the same as every other home on the street. A rockery, three tall conifers and a netted bay window hid what was going on between the married couple. Chloe pounced into action. Billy was barely over the shag pile, into the living room and onto her draylon sofa. There wasn't time for him to draw breath before Chloe flung him on his back, ripped open his shirt, and pulled down his leathers. She slid out of her Lycra and on top of him. God, this woman felt good and tasted even better. She rode him like a bucking bronco whilst pushing his hands over her hot breasts. This unquenched demon writhed relentlessly on top of his slender body. Every thick inch of him surged deeper into her. Fucking hellfire. Salty heat dripped. Electric. He bit his bottom lip. Hair yanked. Moaning, writhing, moaning, writhing. Skin slapped. Panting. Screaming. Yes. More. Yes. More. Breathe. Billy lay mesmerised as they both pulled their head off the papered ceiling. Chloe laughed, stroked the wet locks from his face, and kissed him. And in that soggy moment, she had baptised him into manhood. He was purified.

The very next morning, he opened his wardrobe door and ripped the clothes off their plastic hangers. He was a man and men didn't wear girl clothes. No, these weren't even fit for the charity shop either. He grasped hold of the bin liner containing his sin and discretely threw them into the large industrial bins behind the halls before anyone realised what he was doing. Chloe would be disgusted if she found out. He had never been happier to purge away his past. Over the six months, his four times-a-week romp with Chloe turned into a journey of sexual discovery. And both were willing to go along for the ride. Beep-Beep-Beep- Beep signified the end of Newcastle's version of rewriting the 'Joy of Sex' textbook. Billy stood at the hole in the wall and prayed for the cash machine to give him some doe. Even pleading with the bank manager was fruitless. Chloe couldn't help him out either. Whilst Billy was good for a roll, she certainly didn't want to buy the whole haystack. There were plenty more students in the sea to catch. With no money, there was no university course and no future. With his tail firmly between his legs, Billy returned home to find his parents were also going their separate ways.

His father grunted over the local rag, "If you want to stay here, then you'll have to find yourself a job and sharpish too. You've had your chance at university and blown it. Welcome to the real world, Billy. You'll have to pay your own way. Especially with your mother leaving me for that dickhead she met at the video store. Every penny counts now. There's no money for luxuries or any other extravagance. Do you understand what I am saying, son?"

"Yes, Dad, it's crystal clear to me. I met a wonderful woman in Newcastle who taught me what being a man is about." Billy felt a ball and chain locked around his foot.

"Good, as long as we're clear where you stand. I heard the nurses talking at the Eastfield the other week when I was servicing the radiators. They're looking for staff. Give the ward manager a call. I think his name is Max. He seemed like a decent bloke when I was there last week. Mention me when you call and see what happens."

"Alright Dad, I will and thank you", Billy said as he pulled his lead weight behind him.

---

Poppy and I thumbed through the candidate's details before calling the next one in. It hadn't seemed like five minutes since I'd been at the receiving end of all of this. And now I had my own office; not that I wanted it anymore. But this certainly wasn't the time or place for any of that. There was work to be done. I smiled as she fidgeted in the chair next to me. "You know Poppy, it was Carla who shone Florence's lamp at me in the first place. I was in awe of her, back in the day. That bit hasn't changed, I still am. She was a nurse in A and E and I was a domestic assistant when we first met. Without her, I wouldn't be here today."

"That's lovely to hear, Max, it really is. What did she do?"

"She took me under her wing and made me believe in myself. She pointed me towards health care assistant training. I wasn't very confident back then, you see. And whilst she was recovering from her boob job, she even wangled herself to be my assessor on my first ward. I owe her so much, I do."

"What, she had a boob job? Well, I never," she laughed. And with that, I opened the door and welcomed in the next interviewee for the position of health care assistant within my ward.

The young man had made an effort, which is more than I could say for some of the previous candidates who looked like they were taking the bins out rather than applying for a career within the NHS. You only get one chance to make a first impression after all. He wore a crisp white shirt, pale blue tie and a beautifully fitted grey suit. His long blonde locks were tied back, uncovering a pair of baby blue eyes and a cleanly shaven face. A hint of, but not overpowering, aftershave wafted in my direction as he leaned forward and firmly gripped my hand. There were no rings on his long fingers. He smiled and said,

"It's good to see you again, Mr Austin. Thank you for inviting me to interview and also for allowing me to visit the ward the other day. It helped me get on board with the excellent work that goes on here. I'd be grateful if you'd consider me for the position."

Impressed by his boldness but equally aware that there was a strict and impartial interview procedure to follow, I replied, "Just hold on a minute, Billy. While I admire your enthusiasm, we need to begin the formal questioning and score you fairly in line with every other applicant today. I hope you understand.

"We've met before, but let me introduce you to one of my most experienced nurses; Poppy. I'll kick off the questions, and she'll continue. If you need any clarity, then please stop us and we'll phrase the questions differently. Just try to relax. We want to bring out the best in you. I'll phone you later with the outcome and feedback. I see that we have your contact number on the application form. Will you be available to receive a call this evening?"

Billy smiled, adjusted his lapel and said, "Yes, I will, thank you."

And to be completely honest, he cakewalked the questions, giving responses that were better than some candidates who had previous care experience. This young man was ambitious, receptive to change, and completely patient-focused. His previous informal visit to the ward had paid dividends. Poppy and I agreed he was the right fit for our team. One of the nicer but rare parts of being a ward manager is to deliver good news. It was an absolute pleasure to welcome Billy to the Eastfield family. Maybe it was the bad line, but I could've sworn I heard a muffled cry when I offered him the job.

# Chapter Ten

Decisions, decisions, decisions. Maria swung open the perfectly appointed cubby above her kettle and finally settled for chamomile and fennel. Yes, detox and calm were perfect for this time of the evening. After all, she had gone for gold at the yoga class earlier in the day. Never in her wildest dreams was the 'downward facing dog' or a cupboard brimming with herbal tea on the menu. But you never know what is just around the corner. With the cup steaming in her hand, she waltzed through her beautiful kitchenette. These beechwood cabinets were far easier to keep clean than that shaker-style kitchen in her former Victorian pile. Not that cleaning was ever on the top of the agenda. Life was just too short. Her reflection smiled back to her from the frameless mirror that hung in pride of place in the open-plan lounge diner. This Scandinavian chic was perfect. It was less about chucking out the chintz and more about emptying her head. In about four seconds flat, she was sitting at her favourite perch on the balcony. With views of the high street and Queens Park, it was the perfect spot to sit and watch the world go by before bed. The street lights and fluorescent bar signs mesmerised her. It would look even better at Christmas when the decorations were lit. Brrrr. She pulled her light brown teddy bear dressing gown closer and admired the delicacy of a white patio rose. Whilst unconsciously rubbing a hand through a pot of lavender, a gruff voice bellowed below, "Good Evening Maria. It's a cool evening, isn't it?"

"Oh, Sorry Len, I was a million miles away. It certainly is," she said whilst pulling the dressing gown shut, "have a good evening and a safe journey home. You must be knocking off now."

"Yes, I am, Maria. I'll be back in the morning if you need anything, though. John is on the night shift."

Maria waved whilst counting her blessings. It was certainly worth every penny of the monthly service charge to know that there was twenty-four-hour security in the complex of apartments. Even though the town was relatively safe, this was just the cherry on the cake. There were so many activities covered in the service charge too. She was a regular at the steam room, gym and now yoga classes. Who would've thought it? Whilst the intention was never to lose weight, Maria had already dropped three dress sizes. And this alone fuelled regular shopping expeditions to the high street. It'd taken a while, but she felt like herself again. And even better than any of this, it wouldn't be long before she was going to be a nanny. Although her herbal cup of tea was now half empty, her life certainly wasn't.

True to his word, Len was back on duty the next morning and sitting in the goldfish bowl. His brown eyes twinkled from behind the security glass when he saw her. No matter how many times he had told her, Maria couldn't get her head around the swipe thingy. She fumbled with a rather large black handbag and yet another carrier bag full of baby clothes. But her nemesis had won again. Len smirked at the spectacle and rose from his cockpit. "Let me help you, Maria. It must be the door."

"Thanks, yes, that must be it, Len. It has nothing to do with the fact that I'm as clumsy as a donkey, is it? You should've seen me on my first morning in the bank when I was just a mere slip of a girl. I almost fell up the steps and into the lobby. What a way to make an entrance."

"I would've liked to see that. I don't mean your fall though."

"Are you flirting with an old girl now?" Maria felt a red rash suddenly creeping under her silk collar.

"You see, just because we aren't sixteen anymore, doesn't mean that our lives are over, does it?"

Maria looked at the man standing in front of her, doing his best to charm the birds out of the trees. And it was working. She couldn't get her head around Len's interest in her though. Her marriage to George had seen to that. Yet, here was this smirking stocky greying man in his blue scruffy jumper and bobbled trousers, making her feel things that she hadn't felt in years. And she loved it. He was right; just because they were older didn't mean that they should just curl up and die. Maria loitered in the now open doorway, wondering how to fill the pregnant pause. Somehow, a mooch around town didn't seem as appealing as it did ten minutes ago. Choosing her words carefully, she said,

"Yes, you're right Len. I'm sure that some people think that anyone over sixty needs to be put out to pasture."

He wiped his hands down the side of his bobbles and shuffled from foot to foot. "Well, in that case, shall we prove them wrong? Would you care to go out for a spot of supper one evening? My treat, of course."

"I'd love to Len. That sounds wonderful." And with that, she almost skipped out of the door, under the subway and onto the high street. Dorothy had nothing on her, with or without that annoying scarecrow and stupid lion. But what would she wear?

Maria may have been flicking through the rails in her favourite boutique on the hunt for the perfect outfit, but her mind was elsewhere. Not even Liberace tinkling in the background could focus her thoughts. Len was like a bolt from the blue. But after George, she thought that nonsense was well and truly behind her. And yet, here she was, looking for a size fourteen dress that said 'elegant but not trying too hard'. Just as she was on the verge of giving up, a blouson sleeve chiffon number with the occasional embroidered sequin caught her attention. That would look perfect with a simple string of pearls and a matching clutch bag. Now, where were the bags?

With her jet-black hair blow-dried into a long bob, the lightest touch of make-up and her dress fitting like a glove, she waited in her hallway. Why on earth did she feel like a teenager all over again? She stood in front of the hall mirror, hardly recognising the reflection frowning back at her. The woman she knew was a rippling has-been. Len's timing was impeccable. And oh my goodness, didn't he scrub up well? Out were the bobbles and in was a herringbone jacket, white linen shirt, a pair of cream chinos and brown brogues. Even his greying hair was trimmed into a stylish side parting. He smelt as good as he looked too. A hint of burnished spice replaced his usual oily odour. Yum. Why hadn't she noticed this man before? But then again, she hadn't been in the market for romance.

"Wow Maria, you look stunning. Thank you for agreeing to go out with me. That shade of blue looks beautiful on you."

She looked down and laughed. "You mean this old thing?" And with a hop, skip and a jump, the couple were through the entrance door, under the subway and onto the high street. Maria hadn't even realised that she had linked him until they were standing outside of the restaurant. But even this felt good.

Frankie Valli warbled in the background as the couple took their place at a pretty red and white gingham-covered table. It wasn't the most sophisticated choice, but in all honesty, it didn't need to be either. Len was lucky to get a table at short notice as the quality of the food spoke for itself. But after pulling a few strings with Giovanni, a table was found in an intimate corner at the back of the restaurant. Len pulled the chair out for his date and steadied a red candle that was dripping over a wine bottle. There was always the vintage Americana to talk about if need be. It was hard to see where the walls ended and this priceless collection began. Giovanni only meant to stay in the United Kingdom for a couple of weeks sightseeing, but the allure of cheese and bacon oatcakes and, of course, his Sarah had tempted him over the pond. As he often said to his guests as he seated them, his wife would never know if it was the oatcakes or her that had swung the deal. Even after all of these years of running the pizzeria together, that joke never got old. A candle-lit black-and-white photo of Elvis wearing a studded jumpsuit gyrated over proceedings.

Maria peered at the photo. "Oh, look, Len. It shows him singing 'Suspicious Minds' at the International Hotel. Gosh, he looked so happy then, didn't he? No one had any idea what was going on behind that quiff. That Colonel Sanders chap wasn't exactly a nice man."

"It's so sad what was happening behind his smiles. Such a waste of a wonderful life. Thank you for agreeing to go out with me. Life is too short for regret, isn't it?"

From behind the flickering candlelight, Maria said, "It certainly is. The pleasure's all mine."

Sarah creaked over the dark wood floorboard, pulled a pen out of her blonde bun, and smiled. "It's so lovely to see both of you again, and especially together. You may not know this, Len, but without Maria, we wouldn't have been able to open this place. I can remember it as if it was yesterday. Giovanni and I were so nervous when we went to see Mrs Taylor at the bank.

"It's not every day that you get time with the bank manager. It's easier to get an audience with the Pope. But within five minutes of meeting, we were all chatting like old friends. I can still see Margaret Thatcher staring out from her frosty frame above Maria's head. God, I hated that woman; I mean Margaret. She was a mean old bat. Maria believed in us when no one else would. And she was right, Giovanni's Chicago Pizzas have trail-blazed other restaurants.

"And let's not forget your kindness too, Len. I don't know what we would've done without you. If you hadn't stepped in and sorted out that burst pipe, our New Year takings would've been ruined. It's hard to run a restaurant with a tidal wave lapping from the kitchen. But enough about my trip down memory lane. What can I get you both?"

It wasn't long before the conversation was flowing as easily as the wine. But Maria had learnt the hard way to know when enough was enough. Like Lady and the Tramp, the couple were happy to share a meal. But there was no spaghetti to slurp. Instead, they plumped for a large pepperoni pizza between them. The food was simple, but delicious. In between trying to catch mozzarella cheese strings before they landed on his new shirt, Len said,

"So Maria, tell me all about you. I've noticed a young man and an attractive lady who I assume to be his wife visiting you regularly. The lady is heavily pregnant. Am I right in thinking that they are your son and daughter-in-law?"

"Correct Sherlock. That's my Christian and his lovely wife, Carla. He's a doctor at the City Infirmary and Carla usually works as a junior sister at the Eastfield Hospital."

"Oh, did you say the Eastfield? Well, it's a small world, isn't it? I know it well. I used to work in maintenance at the City Infirmary and often went to the Eastfield to service the radiators and heating. My son

Billy works on a ward as a health care assistant there. I wonder if he knows your Carla? I'll ask him when I see him."

"I see. She might well know him. Does he live with you?" Her heart raced under her new dress. What if Len already knew about her less-than-perfect past? But why would he ask her out then? After all, her ex-husband had worked at the City Infirmary for years. And in that candle-flickering, Elvis-watching moment, the penny dropped. She wanted Len's approval for some strange reason. He mattered.

"Until recently, he lived with me. He's shacked up with some woman he's met at work now. Before he went, it was just me and him since his mother left. She swanned off with a younger model from the video shop. It turned out she was exchanging more than videotapes. But that's water under the bridge now."

"How lovely. You must be so proud of your son," Maria tactfully replied, whilst thinking the date was over before it had started. It would only take a few minutes for Len to join the dots. But instead, he shocked her.

Len couldn't work out what had changed. All he knew was that the atmosphere had nose-dived from Disney to Hammer House in less time than it took to gulp a mouthful of merlot. Oh, well, in for a penny, in for a pound. There's nothing like the truth. And if Maria didn't like it, then it wasn't far from the taxi rank. He looked at her directly in the eyes and puckered his chest. "Truthfully, Maria, I'm not going to lie to you. I've been a terrible father in the past. "

Phew, he doesn't know. She turned her head slightly and sipped her wine. "Who's perfect, Len? My ex-husband and I were dreadful parents. He was a Consultant Oncologist at the hospital. His name is George. Are you aware of him? I'm doing my best to make up for lost time with Christian before it's too late."

Len frowned and leaned a little closer to his date until he could almost taste her breath. "You mean that snooty good-for-nothing so-and-so who walked around with his nose in the air? Well, I never. I knew who he was, but he never acknowledged us low life. And now I am worried too. I'm so sorry, but what do you mean by 'while you still have the time'? Are you dying, Maria?"

"No, no, sorry. I don't mean that. I had a younger son named Jack. He died from the complications of a head injury before I had the chance to make peace with him. There isn't a day that goes by that I don't deeply regret everything. And now it's too late to say that I am sorry and that I love him. George and I were monsters. He was gay, and we turned our back on him."

"Maria, I'm no one to judge. Trust me. Well, I suppose at least we've cleared the air if nothing else tonight," he said, shrugging from his side of the table.

As much as Len and Maria insisted, Sarah was having none of it. She even called her husband out from the kitchen for reinforcement. This meal was definitely on the house. Sarah's eyes twinkled as she looked at the photograph above their table and said,

"Now look, with Elvis as my witness, how many more times do I have to tell you that your money is no good here tonight?

I'll tell you what, when you two lovebirds get married, then put me down to have the wedding reception here. At a push, we can sit up to seventy-five people. Better still, go to Vegas, get married by Elvis himself and come back here for the reception. I've been watching you from over my pinny all night. There's definitely a lot of 'love me tender' going on."

How could they reply to that? The couple left hand in hand with Sarah's teasing ringing in their ears. The glow of orange streetlights and a car park aren't the most romantic of locations, but Len thought sod it. Whilst helping Maria to open her security door again, he leaned in and kissed her on her cheek. And to his utter amazement, she turned and placed a peck on his lips. Goodness me, where had that come from? There was life in the old dog, after all. It was probably just as well they both had been at the garlic bread. Maria waved goodnight and pranced through the corridors. No, this time she would take the stairs rather than the elevator. With a steaming hot cup of fennel tea in her hand, she took up her perch on the balcony. There was certainly a lot of thinking to do.

# Chapter Eleven

Julie lay in the mutual squelch and tried to make out what the silhouette was doing in the corner of their bedroom. After emptying his bag, he jumped up without even a kiss or a cuddle. And although she didn't mind lying on her front, just once, she would've liked to see his eyes for a change. But beggars couldn't be choosers. She'd been lucky to snare such a handsome man in the first place. Julie never forgot what her ex-boyfriend had called her before he left. Those encephalitic words still infected her mind. And as much as Billy had told her she was beautiful, she still felt like a fat lump that no amount of acyclovir could heal. The strange combination of their earlier shenanigans mixed with gloss paint hit the back of her throat. It was just a pity that it was wasted in the darkness. In her mind's eye, she imagined the freshly painted crimson walls with stencilled golden angel wings above their headboard, contrasting crisp white paintwork and the new pine bedroom suite. Oh well, it would still be there in the morning.

If she lived to be one hundred, Julie would never understand what he wanted with her dowdy-dinner lady physique. He could do so much better than her. She pulled the long black hair from her eyes and ran her finger up and down the ruby silk sheets. A wry smile crept upon her face as she thought of the wisecracks that they had shared when she served Billy lunch at the Eastfield. It was always something to do with her battering his sausage or slapping his spotted dick. Never in her wildest dreams did she think it would come to anything more than that. When he leaned over the fryer and asked her out, she thought he was playing some cruel joke. But her name wasn't Carrie, there was no bucket of pig's blood above her head and he meant every word. And before she knew it, he had somehow moved into her stone-clad two-bed terrace on the edge of the city.

Being so close to the centre of town had its advantages. The shops, bus station and library were all within spitting distance. Billy loved window shopping, and she was more than happy to go along with him. Julie somersaulted to her back on the bedsheets and tried to get comfortable. She grabbed for a tissue in the dark, gave her bits a quick wipe, and propped herself up against the pine headboard. It was a real art to have a sneaky slurp of something warm without so much as a clink. It had been worth every penny to have those silent draw runners fitted on their bedside lockers. Gulp. Perfect, that felt better. And with a quick spray of breath freshener, no one would be any the wiser.

Good god, he was fiddling in the corner of the bedroom again. What was the fascination with that computer? Billy played with that more than he did her. He wouldn't try to dial-up internet porn whilst she was in the same room, would he? That'd be like rocking up to a 'Take That' gig, sitting in the car and listening to a tape of the band instead of going through the doors. As she cleared her throat, his silhouette quickly swivelled towards her and then back to the screen. And with that, he suddenly powered down his tortured Dalek instead of dialling it up. At least he was getting their money's worth out of their technology bundle, even if the hire purchase plan was crippling. The next thing she saw was his slim figure grabbing her Chinese silk dressing gown and slinking out of the room. How he got down those steep terrace stairs in the middle of the night without so much as a candle to stop him from falling was a miracle in itself.

Moonlight shone through the frosted bathroom window as Billy sized himself up in the mirror. But even this ethereal haze couldn't hide how he felt. The immersion heater trundled into life and rattled the pipes into action. As the water gushed into the tub, he slowly lowered his mottled body into the lavender bubbles and sighed. Now that the smell of sin was gone, it was time to unwind. He watched the condensation on the window form intricate patterns as he lay in the darkness until his mind settled. These terraced houses were perfect. Julie was probably in the land of nod by now. There was no way that she'd attempt to navigate the steep stairs, wade through the emerald back living room, dive into the galley kitchen and pass the drafty back door to get to him unless something was drastically wrong. And having a separate toilet just off their bedroom in a former cubby hole meant he was safe in his steamy solitude. She thought he was stupid. But it was just easier to ignore the half bottles of vodka that were stored in the toilet cistern, under their bed and at the bottom of her wardrobe. Who indeed was he to judge?

For a few minutes, he closed his eyes and immersed himself under the waterline, with only his nose and mouth exposed. Ther-dump, ther-dump, ther-dump, ther-dump. There was something about hearing his heartbeat echo through the water that always calmed him. As much as he tried, these feelings weren't going anywhere soon. Finding that there were other people online who felt the same way only made it harder to suppress. And having sex, if you could call it that, with Julie, didn't make it go away either. If only she hadn't got wasted the night before. He could still hear her slurred words in his head. Why had that silly woman told all their friends that they were getting married? It was just a pity that she hadn't asked him first. And now he was stuck. But what was the alternative? He couldn't go home to daddy dearest and admit failure.

Julie looked almost beautiful in her fuchsia twin piece and matching fascinator. Billy had done a great job of helping to pick it out for her. The sales assistant in their favourite department store almost fawned over them when she found out it was for a bridal outfit. After a quick phone call to her store manager, she even passed on her twenty per cent staff discount to the happy couple. Well, the young, handsome groom was one of her best customers. It was just a pity that he got his young wife's dress size so wrong. There was no way she was a ten to twelve on any day of the week. Julie clutched a fake flower bouquet in her hand and her groom in the other as they stomped up the aisle. The dulcet tones of Abba's 'I-do, I do, I do, I do' rang from the tape deck. Billy thought 'Bat Out of Hell' would've been more fitting as he was frogmarched to the registrar. He felt ridiculous in the hired grey morning suit. But Julie had insisted on it. After all, it was only a quick registrar office job and not a re-enactment of Prince Charles and Lady Di's wedding. And just look at what had happened to them. But at least there weren't any real people at this shambles, with only two of Julie's drinking friends there as witnesses. After the obligatory I do's, a quick handful of confetti, and a few pictures taken on the steps with a disposable camera, it was over. The happy couple retreated with a takeaway curry to the comfort of their home to enjoy a romantic night by candlelight.

A holiday would do them both good, and this new-fangled internet was just the ticket to research the possibilities. With the World Wide Web at her fingertips, Julie dialled up the computer. Whilst it loaded, she hung out a load of washing, wiped over the kitchen sides, cleaned the takeaway from the night before, made herself a brew and returned to the bedroom. By the time her husband would have finished his shift at the Eastfield, she intended to have dates, prices and locations all sorted. She settled into the swivel cock pit and waited eagerly to explore the endless options that were out there. As the pixels became clearer, the taste of vomit rose in her throat like battery acid. And this had nothing to do with the curry or the vodka, either. How could that bastard do this to her? After all that she had done for him. And more to the point, who the fuck was Michelle?

Billy could sense that something was wrong as soon as his key turned in the door. Julie normally waited for him downstairs after his shift. He knew she had the hump because he went to work the day after they had tied the knot. But as he tried to explain to her, the NHS doesn't stop for man nor beast. And anyway, admitting to Max that he was getting married would cause all sorts of craziness that he wasn't ready to own. Getting married was bad enough as it was without having his face rubbed in it. The last thing he wanted was to parade Julie around like a prize pig at a ward wedding shower. He picked up his jacket, hung it on the hook, and chilled at the dining table, staring at the fish tank. Two pale pink kissing fish were sucking the lips off each other. Whilst they looked like they were kissing, they were actually involved in an aggressive battle with their mouths. The jewelled Siamese fighter was his favourite fish. This peacock-coloured slender beauty with long wispy fins looked so innocent. This elegant loner couldn't exist with another male in the same tank as they would fight until one of them perished. The female was such a brown dowdy thing in comparison. Indeed, people in their native country would cruelly pit the male fish against each other, just like in cock fights.

Billy moved through the pale blue front dining room and into the emerald lounge. Despite the imprint of her bottom on the velvet-sagging sofa, there was still no sign of his bride. He stuck his head into the galley kitchen and noticed a line of washing blowing in the backyard. And then he clicked. After doing a load of washing, Julie had gone for a well-earned rest. She had more than her fill of vodka last night and probably needed to sleep it off. Just as he was loading another batch of whites into the washer, he heard her voice calling him. As he entered the hot crypt, she spun on the swivel chair like the demon in the Exorcist film. With the same malevolence, she spat,

"Who the fuck is Michelle, you dirty fucking bastard?"

"What are you on about? I've just come in from work. What the fuck is wrong with you now?"

"There is nothing wrong with me, you fucking lying twat. Look at this screen. You've been talking to this girl in a fucking chat room named Michelle. I'm not fucking stupid, you lying little git. What the fuck?"

Billy's world dropped out of the bottom of his gut. He could continue to lie to her or just come clean. Either way, he was screwed. But at least she would know the truth, and for some reason, that mattered. "Just listen to me, Julie. You're not going to like it. I'm not having sex with other women."

"Yes, sure, you think I'm stupid. You men are all the fucking same."

Billy took a deep breath, backed off a little in fear of her remaining slipper and said, "Michelle is trans. This is a trans chat room where we meet and support each other."

"We?"

"Yes, 'We'. I'm trans. I always have been and always will be, even before I knew there was a word to describe how I feel inside."

"Oh, the fucking hell fire. I wasn't expecting that."

"Do you want me to leave? I've hurt you enough."

Julie looked up from her blubbering mess and sobs, "Billy, I don't know what I want. But stay for now, at least. We need to talk. I promise not to swear at you anymore. Thank you for telling me the truth."

Following lots of talking and a little drink, everything was finally out in the open. Julie's eyes were like saucers when Billy revealed her true self. But she didn't laugh at Laura, even if her cheap nylon bobbed brunette wig, overdone make-up and black lace dress were all wrong. No, in that moment of desperation, Julie knew exactly what she needed to do. And for the first time in her life, Laura was safe. The pair of them had never been closer. They shopped till they dropped in the department stores together, hand in hand. They spent hours going through endless racks of clothes until Laura had found her sense of style for both day and nighttime. Julie taught Laura how to apply make-up for any occasion, how to dress appropriately for the situation, and how to walk like a lady. Whilst Julie may have lost her Billy, she had a much closer connection with Laura. In return, Laura turned a blind eye to the men who sometimes would inadvertently end up in the marital bed where Billy had once slept. Their marriage may have been over, but their relationship wasn't.

Whilst all this was well and good in the privacy of their two-bedroom terraced home, Laura yearned for freedom. She couldn't live this double life anymore. Something had to give. On a busy Tuesday afternoon at the Eastfield Hospital, Billy decided that enough was enough. Plucking up the courage, he banged on his boss's door.

"Whatever is the matter with you, Billy? You look like you've seen a ghost. Come here and sit down before you fall. Are you not well?" I said, looking at the pasty young man hyperventilating on the chair next to me.

"Max, Max, I-"

"-Whatever's the matter, Billy. Are you in trouble? What can I do to help you? You're worrying me. Just calm down, have a sip of water, and tell me. There's nothing we can't fix together," I said, passing him a plastic cup from the water dispenser.

Following a moment of quietness, he shook his golden locks and said, "Max, I think you will understand, and that is why I've come to you."

"Understand what, Billy, please tell me." I was thinking about all sorts of stuff. What had he done?

"Well, you see Max, I got married to a great woman a few months ago. Her name is Julie."

"Is that it, you dark horse? Half of the female staff here will be devastated, and the other half will be relieved. There are no worries, Billy. I'll just process the forms with Human Resources to ensure that Julie is listed as your next of kin. When you are ready, you can tell the team. Congratulations."

"No, Max, will you let me finish for a change? Please listen. Julie has been helping me with my transition to my true self. Ever since I was a child, I knew I had been born into the wrong body. I want to come to work as the person who I know I am deep down. I want to live full time as Laura."

"I'm sorry. I was completely wrong about that. I get it now. I keep on saying that in my ward and my wider NHS family, we're all equally welcome. And I mean that with all of my heart.

"I won't try to pretend that I understand what you've been going through. But just know that I'll do everything in my power to support you. We'll go at your pace. Just give me your permission to discuss this with Eunice, Jan and Shirley. They're great people and will be as supportive as me."

"Yes, of course, no problem. I guess the staff will need to be briefed too."

"They will, but you'll be at the centre of this. You're the most important person here."

"Thank you, Max, you're one in a million. Something told me you would understand."

"Well, you see, without me going into detail, I know what it feels like to be ostracised by cruel bullies. Trust me, some nurses don't live up to the title. I certainly won't stand for any of that crap here, I promise you that."

And although I had shared a little more than I had intended, it felt right. How could I expect Laura to bring her entire self to work if she felt her manager was not willing to do the same? For years, I'd hidden my story in fear of bigotry, bullying, and hate. Just sweep it under the carpet and forget about it. No one will be interested, anyway. Laura was the bravest person I had ever met. It may have taken her a while to get there, but at least she could look people in the eye and say,

"Like it or lump it, this is who I am."

It was just too bad I couldn't say the same about me. What bloody hypocrisy!

# Chapter Twelve

Serendipity caught me out. The ward phone echoed over the clatter of plates and the smell of minced beef, but I just couldn't get to it. As the only qualified nurse on duty, everything would and could wait unless it was life-threatening. My priorities were making sure that all the patients had their evening medication on time. This was no mean feat in itself, considering most of them were on at least six or seven tablets each. Getting Doreen to take her medication in the first place was tricky at the best of times. It just wasn't her fault. Why would she want to take bitter-tasting tablets when she couldn't remember her name or where she was? That was just too upsetting. Laura sidled up to me as I tried to give Doreen her vital warfarin. Before thinking, I glanced up at her and said,

"I'm sorry, I can't talk now. I'm doing my best to get these pills out, and I need to concentrate."

But Laura was going nowhere. "You need to take this call, Max. I picked up the receiver on my way to dish the food. I'll watch your medication trolley for you, but don't forget to lock it first."

"OK, Ok. I'm coming. Let me just finish signing for Doreen's medication, and then I'll lock the trolley. Guard it with your life whilst I'm gone. I won't be a minute."

The phone was flashing on hold when I got to the nurses' station. Mercifully, I could hide behind it. No one needed to see the ward manager cry. It only took Shirley ten minutes to get to the ward and take over the late shift. The good thing about being a 'hands-on' Matron was that she could jump in whenever. There was no point in asking for cover from the other wards, as we were all on the same sinking ship. Whilst still buttoning up her uniform, I gave a quick hand-over of care and threw her the ward keys. I could feel her hand on my shoulder, as she said,

"Just go, Max, before it's too late. Phone me when you can, but don't worry about this place."

I couldn't remember getting from the Eastfield to the City Infirmary. But somehow my car had landed in a parking spot near the Accident and Emergency Department. I stomped through the rickety automatic doors and gulped down my tears. The familiar mix of bloody bandages, hospec, and plaster of Paris hung in the air. A crackly speaker barked out orders over the proceedings. 'Porter to cubicle three, doctor to the square, emergency team to resus'. I sprinted over to the reception desk. "Where is he, Glenys? Please let me through to the back."

"Max, he's in the resus bay. Let me buzz you through."

Right Max, keep it together. You can do this. My eyes landed on Aunt Bren hovering outside a cubicle opposite the central nursing station. Within a second, I felt her arms around me. Not even her familiar heavy perfume and make-up offered any comfort tonight. She juddered in my arms. "Oh Max, thank god you're here. One minute we were walking Pongo and chatting and the next, he was on the floor. The only blessing was that we were still on the estate.

"That man must've thought that I was mad as a hatter when I banged on his piggin' door. I almost fell on top of the poor soul as it opened and I begged him to call an ambulance. He's not right about

Max. He can't speak properly and his arm and leg won't work. It happened so quickly."

I hugged her a little tighter than usual. Wet make-up covered my left cheek, but I didn't care. "What would I do without you, Aunt Bren? I dread to think what would have happened otherwise."

She shook her head, reliving the trauma in her mind. "Me too. It doesn't bear thinking about. I put him in the recovery position and covered him with my fluffy coat. I have never been so bloody pleased to see an ambulance in all of my life. There was just enough time to drop Pongo off before I dived into the back of it. The poor dog was whimpering like hell."

"Thank you for everything. If you're tired, then please go home and get some rest. You'll be due your painkillers soon. "

"Nonsense, I'm going nowhere and anyway, the pills are in my bag. I'll wait here whilst you go in and sort things out."

"Thanks darling, but please have a seat or something, will you?"

"Stop worrying about me, Max, and go to Wayne. He needs you now more than ever." And she was right. Wayne needed me, but as his partner and not his nurse.

I swished past the curtains and into the cubicle, where I found a stocky ginger-haired staff nurse completing a set of neurological observations. With her pen torch now firmly in her pocket, she smiled through her green and brown flecked eyes and said,

"It's Max, isn't it? You won't recognise me now, but I was a student of yours, many years ago when you worked on the neuro-science wards. My name is Paula, and I'm the nurse in charge of these cubicles."

Why did I need to know half of her life story now? Had I taught her nothing? "Oh- er, hello. What is going on? Sorry, I can't remember you. I've slept since then."

Paula's heart sank. She was only trying to be friendly and look where that had got her. "Right then. We have just come back from an emergency x-ray. The doctor will be in shortly to discuss the scan results. Do you want to sit here? I'll get you and your aunt a cuppa whilst you wait."

Finally, some information. But, I didn't feel like drinking. Right, Max, remember, stiff upper lip and all of that, I thought whilst grabbing hold of Wayne's good hand. The left one just didn't move. But neither did his arm, his leg, or the left side of his face. How could someone so young have a stroke? Every time he tried to speak, incomprehensible sounds slurred from his dry lips. That cubicle was getting smaller by the minute. I gripped his hand and mopped his clammy forehead with a tissue. Then I whispered into the microphone on his hearing aid,

"Just relax darling, your blood pressure is a little high, according to the monitor. Don't worry, you'll be OK. I'll see to that."

There is one thing saying the right thing, but believing it yourself is a whole new kettle of fish. There was only one thing that I was certain about; I was going nowhere. On autopilot, I stroked his hair, dabbed his grazed face with a crumbling tissue and waited for the doctor. A few minutes later, neurologist Dr Desmond Smith arrived on the scene. I had not seen this giant haystack of a man since he had been a junior doctor. But all the same, it was great to see a familiar face, even if his breath did reek of fags. He gripped hold of my hand, almost shaking my shoulder out of its socket, and said in his Jamaican accent,

"Max, I thought it was you. Good to see you after all of these years. We've arranged for Wayne to be transferred to the Neuro-science Unit whilst we figure out what is going on. As you probably are already aware from looking at him, our clinical findings are sadly suggesting a stroke.

"I think we're going to have to complete a few more investigations though, and maybe an MRI scan. Try not to worry Max, he's in good hands. I'll do everything I can to get to the bottom of all of this sorry lot. You have my word."

Well, that was asking the impossible. "Thank you, Desmond, I know you will. I just can't get over it. He's only young, he doesn't smoke, and is fit as a flea. I've no idea what has caused this."

I wish I'd a pound for every time that I'd greeted upset relatives through those heavy ward doors. And now it was our turn to be on the receiving end. On one hand, I was extremely grateful that he had landed within Sharron's Varley's ward as I knew Wayne would receive excellent care. But on the other, we hadn't exactly parted on the best of terms. Well, what goes around comes around. With heart monitors racing as fast as my own, we were ushered into one of the few side rooms next to the nurse's station. It was awkward having a nursing assessment completed by someone you knew. It was a bit like wrapping your own present up and acting surprised on Christmas morning. But needs must when the devil drives. Sister Sue sat opposite us, took a pen from her beehive, grabbed hold of my hand and said,

"It's OK, Max, we'll sort you both out. For once, I can't find the words. But let's go through the process, complete this assessment, and then I will fill in the blanks. You know I have to do it."

"OK, Sue, no worries. I'm just glad that you're on duty. I also appreciate that you have sorted this side room out for us. That's so kind." If only she knew what I was thinking.

She smiled through the same shade of pink lipstick that she had worn for years. "Yes, this is the room where I watched you become a nurse, isn't it? It was the only free one."

"You are all brilliant and I trust you with my life." Wayne's hand trembled in my hand.

"Well, in that case, take the hint. Please go home and let us do our job, Max. You need some rest. But you can come any time."

It was hard to steal away, but Sue was only saying what I had advised countless worried relatives to do. I kissed Wayne's salty lips. "Sue wants me to go now, darling. I'll come back tomorrow. I love you."

He half smiled, tried to kiss me back and mumbled something incoherent in my ear. I picked Aunt Bren up from the relative's room and gave her a moment in private to say her goodbyes. Within ten minutes we were at home, sitting with Pongo wedged firmly between us. He was going nowhere. He tilted his head, whimpered, and settled into my chest. A thousand questions buzzed through what was left of my brain.

Aunt Bren eased Pongo's rear end from her hip. "Max, I know what you're thinking, duck. But just because Jack came out of there in a wooden box, doesn't mean that Wayne will do the same."

Well, she was blunt, if nothing else. "I know that in my logical head, I do. But I just miss him so much. I loved Jack."

"Everyone knows that, Max. And it will be all raked up again now that Wayne is in the same bloody ward too. It couldn't have been any worse, could it? But it only takes a few good people to prop you up and keep you going. There're times when Danni gets on what's left of my shrivelled tits so much with her righteousness. But you know she cares for you just as much as me. Hopefully, Malc will sort her out. She needs a good seeing too.

"Anyway, what I am trying to say is, yes, lean on us. That's what we are here for." She rummaged in her patent leather purple handbag for a few seconds. I counted at least ten bottles of perfume flirt from the lucky dip. She smiled in relief and waved the round make-up compact at me.

"Why on earth are you topping up your face at this time in the morning? It's unnecessary. I couldn't care less. It's only the two of us. Well three, if you count Pongo?" She shook her head at me and tutted in disgust. It was as if I'd asked for her vital statistics.

"Because I can Max, because I can. How do I know that Rodger Moore is not going to knock at the door at any second and whisk me off my feet? I could be his next Pussy Galore," she cackled whilst opening the compact, "oh, the bloody hell, I look like an anaemic panda.

"Why didn't you tell me? I'd be lucky to attract Count Dracula in this state. And look, my face has dripped all over my purple cardy. It'll never be the same again. What a bloody mess! Quick, just give me a minute before you run me home. If we get stopped by a handsome police officer, then I need to be ready, able, and certainly willing."

She grabbed my arm and slowly got out of the passenger seat. After winking, ruffling my hair, and placing a sticky kiss on my cheek, she slowly creaked up the stairs and into her flat. No matter how hard I tried, she just wasn't having it. Aunt Bren was independent, and that was that. I'm just glad that Mrs 'M', one of the domestic supervisors at the City Infirmary was keeping tabs on her. Beneath her green tabard, no-nonsense attitude, and greying hair, she had a heart of gold. It warmed my heart to hear that they gave Aunt Bren the lighter jobs. These days, she had to push nothing heavier than a kex mop or high duster around the back offices and boardroom. Her bones creaked louder than the mortuary door. And both needed regular maintenance to stop them from seizing up.

*Tender love is blind, it requires dedication.* Sleep deprivation and desperation did funny things to my sense of reality as Pongo and I dozed together on the sofa, half listening to a Dolly Parton CD. *All this love we feel needs no conversation.* But this time, when it happened, I wasn't scared or confused. *We ride it together, ah ha. Making love with each other, ah ha.* The leather cushion squeaked, Pongo looked up and waved his tail frantically. *Islands in the Stream, that is what we are.* And then I couldn't hear the music anymore. My beautiful tin soldier was sitting on the sofa next to me. I hadn't seen him look this happy since his opening night with Miss Nancy Eclair as her tambourine-shaking sidekick. But that was a million years ago and everything had changed since then. Was I seeing what I wanted to see, or was it him? Well, if I was delusional, then Pongo was too.

His eyes sparkled in the most heavenly blue that I had ever seen. As if reading my mind, he calmly said,

"Max, don't be frightened. It is really me. Gladys told you I would pop in when you needed me, didn't she? Now listen and please don't interrupt, as I can't stay long. You should've seen what I had to do with St. Peter's organ to be allowed here. Enough of the smut. Let me get to the point. Wayne will be fine. Yes, he has had a stroke and will need time to rehabilitate, but there's no room for him yet with me. He's yours to keep, Max, until you are both ancient and grey. Look after him, you've a lot in store together. An atrial septal defect has caused the stroke. It's not shown up on the scans yet, but a blood clot has passed through a hole between the upper chambers of his heart. It's stopped the oxygen to his brain too. But it can be fixed.

"Make sure you tell the doctors straight away. He was a premature baby, wasn't he? His heart hadn't formed properly. Michael is waiting for me Max, I haven't got long left. He's as kind and beautiful as his brother. Adam is still struggling. Please help him see it wasn't his fault. Just contact him for me, will you? I will always love you. Don't pine for me, I'm happy with Michael. Now I have to go before St. Peter makes me do unspeakable things to him with a French horn."

Through my tears, I just spurted out, "I love you too" before my beautiful Jack in a box moved from this world to the next one again. With every ounce of my heart, I would do exactly what Jack had told me to do. Contacting Nancy out of the blue and telling her that her dead ex had a message for her was one thing in itself, but convincing a hospital team without getting locked up was a whole new ball game. Oh well, in for a penny, in for a pound; there was no time like the present.

Following a quick shower and a change of clothes, I returned to the ward. As I entered through the doors, I caught Sister Sharron Varley's eye. She rose from her throne in the ward manager's office and called me in. It was like time had stood still. If anything, there were even more piles of coloured papers falling off her desk than I remembered. How she found anything was beyond me. My office was clean and organised in comparison. But this wasn't the time to play spot the difference. She patted me on the knee when I slumped down next to her. I couldn't help but notice her annual rugby player calendar above her desk, still in pride of place. She said,

"How are you, Max? That's a silly question, sorry. It's been a long time since you have been in that chair, hasn't it? Let me just be honest with you. I was an absolute cow and shouldn't have done that to you. I, more than anyone, would know exactly what that would do to your confidence."

"When I look back, I'm ashamed. I should've stood up to that bloody director of nursing and told him where to stick it. I was a coward and put my job over your well-being. You know what that man is like. He has his ways and wanted you gone. And that was that. He never thought you'd get a job when you qualified. That ruthless bastard!

"There's not a day that goes by when I don't think about what I did to you. And I just fired his bullets whilst he pulled the trigger in silence. Thank god that he's gone. They promoted him out; I think. But watch out for the new one. She isn't much different. Some sisters here are calling her a smiling assassin. She talks the talk and pretends to be nice, but underneath those blonde locks, she's a witch. Just giving you the heads-up before she makes her way to the Eastfield. I'll take care of your Wayne, just as you took care of the patients when you worked here."

And with that, years of anger floated out of the window as easily as Sharron's filing system. "I appreciate your honesty. But things happen for a reason. I just couldn't see it when I stormed off to London. As you know, I've been a ward manager at the Eastfield for a few years now. I doubt any of that would have happened if I'd got the deputy post here. I didn't know that anything else existed outside of this neuroscience unit. So strangely, you've done me a favour.

"But there's something else that I would like you to do, please. I've dug into Wayne's medical history. And it turns out he has an atrial septal defect. This could have caused his stroke. Can you please make sure that the doctors consult with cardiology immediately? Do this for me and all is forgiven. "

She smiled, jumped into action and stormed from her office to the nurse's station like a tornado, leaving a trail of worried staff in her path. Everyone knew what that strut meant. But this time, I wasn't shaking. I slowly walked behind her, leaving her to it as she waded into Dr Smith's morning ward round. The last thing I heard as I opened the door to greet my man was her dulcet tones drifting over the nurse's station. "Desmond, I've told you the history. Now get one of your performing monkeys here to call the cardiologists immediately. You may be a consultant, but this is my ward and I'm responsible for the nursing care. Do it now."

God, that woman still had it. Just like the City Infirmary, I had fallen in love with her all over again. But that hadn't meant that I had forgotten what they were both capable of. My days of naïve ignorance were well and truly over. And there he was, lying on the crisp white sheets in a pair of starched green pyjamas smelling of hospital soap and baby powder. God knows how I remembered, but somehow I had rounded up a bag of clothes and toiletries from home. His eyes twinkled when he saw me. But even after I had put his hearing aids in properly, only incomprehensible speech came from him. I reminded myself that all of this could be fixed as I kissed his cracked lips. God, did they not routinely complete oral care these days? Standards were slipping.

Within about thirty minutes, he was dressed in a pair of soft jeans and a baggy grey t-shirt, shaved, teeth cleaned, and smelling much more like my man. Just because someone is lying on a hospital bed, doesn't mean that they have to surrender their identity to ritual and routine. My staff at the Eastfield ensured we honoured our patient's sense of identity at all costs. I certainly wasn't settling for anything less here. Knock, Knock, Knock. Dr Smith, his troop of junior doctors, and Sister Sue entered the room. He cleared his throat and said,

"Good morning Wayne, you're looking much better than you did last night. I can see that my nurses have done an excellent job caring for you. We've got a few more scans and blood tests to complete. We've also had a chat with the heart team. They'll be here shortly. If we need to block a hole in your dam, then we will get straight on it. It's amazing. Instead of opening your sternum up like a sardine can, it can be done by keyhole now. I'll sign the medical bit of the consent form for you. Just scribble your signature on the patient section if you agree. You have the capacity to understand everything that I am saying. Our earlier assessments have shown us you do anyhow. You're right-handed, I take it?"

Wayne nodded, signed the form and mumbles something that vaguely sounded like "Thank you" back to him.

He tapped his pockets, jingling their contents. "Excellent. Well, that sounds like a plan then. Oh, and while I'm at it, I forgot to mention that Sharron has agreed to do all the rehabilitation here if that suits you both. As you know Max, we've excellent speech therapy, world-class neurophysiotherapy, and some of the best occupational therapists I've come across at our fingertips. We'll sort everything out. Just trust us."

Angie sat on the end of our sofa, sobbing from under her golden blonde ringlets and blue eye shadow. None of it had anything to do with her, and yet, she blamed herself for everything. It wasn't her fault that Wayne had been born prematurely or the fact that her other son had died in childbirth. We weren't exactly bosom pals, to say the least. And this certainly wasn't the time to tell her that Michael was alive and well in spirit. As much as I tried to explain that Wayne would be fine, she wasn't buying any of my reassurance. I said,

"Look, Angie, I'll tell you what. When we get to the hospital, I'll see if any of the doctors are free to put your mind at rest a little. You're his mother, after all, and you have every right to speak to them. Legally, you're still his next of kin."

By the time I'd pulled up in the hospital carpark, she was in a much better state. Once she had had a chat with the doctors, she even slapped a smile on her face before going to see Wayne. I waited on the familiar leather sofa in the relative's room at the top of the ward whilst she had some alone time with her son. Well, we all couldn't go in at once, and I knew that Aunt Bren and Danni would be on their way at some point too. "I'm here ladies. Great to see you both. Thanks for coming. I'm just waiting for Angie to finish down there."

"But why are you smirking, Max? There's nothing funny about this," Danni said, frowning, whilst Aunt Bren tried to stop the sofa opposite from eating her.

"I suppose I'm thankful for small blessings. For once, Wayne couldn't find an excuse to say 'no' to her visit. We're experts in batting his mother's dramas off. Let me tell you, that woman would make a saint swear. It's always about her. If I have a headache, then she has a migraine. If I have a migraine, then she has a brain tumour. But she won't have any counselling either.

Wayne has asked her time and time again over the years, but he might as well talk to the wall. I know she has had a hard life and terrible things have happened to her, but don't we bloody know it? I'm not hard, I get it. But that woman thinks that the world revolves around her."

Danny giggled and looked at us both. "Say it as it is Sister. You're more like me than I thought. And all this time, Aunt Bren over here thought that I was the mouthy one."

"Oh no, I'm not in your league Danni. But I'll be getting myself a pair of those bloody awful parrot earrings if I'm not careful. How are things going with Malc? Please spill the beans. I need something to take my mind off all of this." And with that, we were gossiping like three fishwives over a garden fence.

"Awe, Max. He's bloody wonderful and nothing like the type of man that I usually go for. Well, for a start, he isn't a bastard. That's always a bonus. He's so thoughtful. Things couldn't be better. When I think about him, I want to smile. He's been like a slow burn."

Bren peered up from her pit. "That man sounds like a keeper. And they're as rare as rocking horse shit. Take my advice and keep hold of him. I had one of those once."

Jack was right, Wayne was fine. I'm not saying his hospital stay was easy for him by any stretch of the imagination though. The pioneering keyhole surgery was a success. This meant that he didn't have to undergo open heart surgery to patch the defect. The Neurologists left no stone unturned to make sure that Wayne had every relevant test and scan available to help his recovery. The nursing and therapy staff worked tirelessly to support my man through the acute and rehabilitation phases of his stroke. I could well and truly feel the City Infirmary's silent thread wrap around us in protective, understated calmness. Aunt Bren, Danni, Christian, Carla, and even Angie pulled out the stops to support me. The Eastfield team couldn't do enough to help either. Jan, Eunice and Shirley adopted an open-door policy, allowing me to come and go as I pleased. Once the staff on my ward learnt of my predicament, they also wrapped their protection around me. Often I found homemade cakes left on my desk from Poppy, our resident master baker. Wayne left the ward with a stick but walking, a slight slur to his voice but speaking, a repaired heart but still breathing. We made adaptations to our house to help him and organised a community rehabilitation program. I couldn't have been any more grateful if I had tried. Something was shifting. My experience at the hands of the NHS was restoring my faith in a system that had left so many deep scars on my very soul.

I hadn't forgotten my promise to my Jack in a box either. But how do you start a conversation with,

"Adam, your dead ex knows that you blame yourself for his death? He's appeared to me a few times and wants you to know that it wasn't your fault. Now, don't worry, just get on with the rest of your life. Oh, and by the way, I'm not making any of this up or going mad."

Wayne and I chewed it all over and hatched a plan. There was no point in trying to catch one of Miss Nancy Eclair's shows in London. Nancy would be thrilled to see us, but there's a right time for everything. And more to the point, she'd hide behind her beautiful beaded lashes and shrug us off with a flippant put-down. But Adam, on the other hand, was sweet and gentle. Yes, that was it; Wayne was just the bait needed to draw him back. I winked at my man, channelled my best drama queen, picked up the receiver, punched in his number and said,

"Hello is that you, Adam? Please tell me it is."

His familiar voice said, "Max, is that your voice? Whatever's wrong?"

"Oh Adam. I've been beside myself. Wayne had a near death experience. He suffered a stroke and ended up being admitted to the same ward as Jack. He's out now. I've been all sixes and sevens. God, I've missed you."

"Oh, my Lord? Is he Ok?"

"He's recovering."

"Right, I'm on my way. Can you pick me up from the station?"

"Thank you. Of course I can." Miss Nancy Eclair wasn't the only person who could put on a show when needed.

I spotted him huddling into a blue Parka jacket on the steps as I pulled up at the train station. It was so good to see him. Miss Nancy Eclair would have air kissed me, but his shivering embrace was real.

It didn't take long before he was warm and sitting in our shabby chic living room, attempting to prevent Pongo from sitting on his beautiful pair of cream moleskin trousers and black t-shirt. The smell of fresh coffee and his favourite French fancies wafted over our hilarity. I just about rescued the tray before Pongo's tail destroyed the lot. Adam's brown hair was trimmed into a side parting. It was just easier to keep it short to slip under a wig cap. He always had very little facial hair, but he'd meticulously plucked what remained of his eyebrows into an elegant curve. Once I had brought him up to speed on all the comings and goings of our motley crew and he had his fill of dog hair and slobber, I spied my moment. "Adam, as you know, Wayne has been sick. But there's another reason we wanted to see you. I don't want to rip the duct tape that is holding your heart together, but it's time to clear the air.

"We know you've run away because you think it's all your fault. But Jack's death had nothing to do with you. It was simply his time to go."

"You've said that to me before. But I don't believe you." A single tear ran over his smooth cheek. Within a few seconds, it was joined by many more.

My head turned sharply. Wayne jumped to my rescue. "Now listen to me, Adam, before I slur again. I wouldn't normally do this, but Jack is telling me you believe in spirit. Your mother still goes to the Spiritualist Church, the one on the main road on the way to town, right? They dragged you there as a kid, too."

Adam sat as stunned as me. He fiddled with the sequined cross that embossed his breast pocket. "Yes, you're right, but how in the world do you know that, Wayne?"

"It's simple. Jack is with us, so please listen to me. I can hear and see him when I tune in. He's fine. No, he's more than fine. He's having a blast in spirit. There was nothing that either you or anyone could've done to stop his death.

"Jack knows I get tired quickly and can't hold this up for long. Go and live your life, go and live your life, go and live your life. Yes, that's what he's trying to say to you. I've just watched him kiss the top of your head and say thank you for loving him. And now he's gone, sorry."

I wasn't sure who was more surprised between the three of us, to be completely honest. Following a silent sip of cappuccino, Adam got up from his chair and ran his hand over the top of his head. I thought he was going to leave. Instead, he came over to our spot on the sofa, put his soggy face between us, and went in for a hug. He said,

"I believe you now. That must've taken a lot out of you Wayne. I'd no idea that you could do that. Thank you so much, both of you. There'll always be some part of me that will blame myself, but this has helped me to make sense of it all. I don't think I can ever return home and work at the European again. It's onwards and upwards for Miss Nancy Eclair."

I felt his ribs shake between us. "I understand, I do. Holding on to a little pain means we can also hold on to a little love, doesn't it? Jack just wanted you to know the truth. There was no way I was going to turn up and tell Nancy this."

His eyes twinkled. "No, I don't blame you. I'm ashamed of the things that she does and says. But as much as I tell her, she won't listen to me. She's a headstrong girl. In fact, Nancy is getting more popular by the minute and is off to Spain in the next few weeks to do a gig in the Canaries. I just wish I had her talent and determination. And speaking of the time, I must get back. My train leaves in an hour. Will you run me to the station?"

"Of course. Please give Nancy our regards. I'd hate her to think we were being rude and excluding her."

"I know she'll be over the moon to hear that I've popped over to see you both and your daft dog. She often talks about you. Now, we really must be getting going. It's been lovely though."

I watched a half-familiar glint of something cross Adam's eyes before he said his goodbyes and left for the station. When I got back, Wayne was curled up with Pongo in the land of nod.

# Chapter Thirteen

Satan scratched his heavy balls, sniffed his salty claw and waited for his next arrival. Placing an out-of-town retail park on a busy road had worked like a treat to ensure a regular stream of fresh souls to stoke his fire. People drove on the dual carriageway like they were on the motorway. It'd been worth every penny to grease the palms of the approval committee. Everyone has a price, after all. The array of glittering chain restaurants, bars, a multiplex cinema, and stores was as good as any red-lit Amsterdam window to tempt the punters in. And it was a stroke of genius to put the biggest baby wear store this side of Manchester in the retail park. Literally, it was like taking candy from a baby.

Why did all the bigger stores have to be in the middle of nowhere? Gone were the days when Carla and Christian could casually stroll through the high street and find baby wear. And ordering from a catalogue is just not the same. You wouldn't buy a car without a test drive, so why would expectant parents feel obliged to order from the glossy pages without checking the quality of the items first? Christian unstrapped his blossoming wife from the tan passenger seat and gently supported her out of their VW Golf. Throughout the whole pregnancy, not once had she moaned or complained. She just got on with the morning sickness, heartburn, stretch marks, and Jack Juniors' nocturnal boxing matches. What a woman. Christian couldn't have loved her anymore. He linked her arm and strolled into the department store. Carla was in heaven. The smell of baby powder hit the back of her throat as she tried to work out which direction she needed to waddle in first.

Shop assistants probably went insane from the constant tinkling of canned nursery rhymes in the background. This place catered to every nesting instinct that any pregnant person could have. With Maria's generous gift burning a hole in the pocket of her pale green maternity dress, Carla's inner warrior princess was unleashed. Jack Junior would have everything and more to greet his arrival in the world. They soon loaded their car with all sorts of essentials. A crib, blankets, a convertible pram, clothes, bedding, toiletries, a bath, a baby alarm system, and disposable nappies were all neatly packaged by the staff. It was a good job that the rear car seats folded down. Carla couldn't wait to stock Jack Junior's powder blue and cream nursery with it all. And Maria would be just as excited to see it in place. She'd been casually filling the room with lots of goodies in the meantime. If anything, this baby business had brought the two women closer together than they'd ever been. And Christian couldn't have been more relieved. His mother seemed genuinely happy these days. He suspected that the still earthiness of Len's influence had something to do with this.

Scraping metal spliced the air. Screech. Bang. Unconsciousness. The last thing they remembered before passing out was clutching hands. There was no time for even an 'I love you'. The side impact of a lorry catapulted them from the carriageway and onto the central barrier. It was over. Darkness. Empty. What was that hiss? Was it a snake wrapping around her face? What was that voice? It didn't sound like Jesus. A blurry image of a man wearing green drifted in. No, Jesus wore white. "Miss, Miss, just keep still. We're cutting you out now. No, don't move. You've been in an accident. Keep still."

Harsh lights floated above her. What were the whirring noises? Why was it blue now? Was there a disco in heaven? Or was this hell? How had she ended up here? A man was prodding at her hand with something sharp. God, that hurt. "No, No, Christian, Christian. "

"I'm right here, darling. We're in the back of an ambulance. A lorry has hit us. Just try to relax." Christian stroked the glass out of his wife's hair as a paramedic simultaneously wrapped a crepe bandage around a laceration to the side of his head.

Carla tried to sit up but was in searing agony. She whimpered "Baby? Christian?"

"Just keep still, my angel. Don't move. We'll be at the hospital in a matter of minutes." And then Christian vomited into a large cardboard bowl. The car and its contents could be replaced. But the three of them couldn't. Indeed, the lorry driver who had side-swiped them on the road to hell could be dealt with in God's good time too. But if Carla and their baby were to survive the impact, then they would require emergency treatment.

The two men sat silently, watching each other in the window's reflection while the train sped away from London. With his head vibrating on the cold window, George tried to smile at Dylan. It was kind of him to drop everything and come running. This exceeded the expectations of their polite conversation in recent weeks. As much as George had enjoyed his quiet game of cat and mouse with him through the coffee houses of Putney, this was pushing it. But when Maria phoned him, George went to pieces. And in reality, there was no-one else to ask for help. Dylan took a sip from his sludge and tapped the table. "George, it's OK. Whatever happens, you are not alone. I'm here. But to be honest, I'm just as nervous as you. I haven't seen Maria since the infamous night of our graduation."

George weighed up the options. This was a fast train and Dylan couldn't get off, right? And it was probably better hearing it from him, anyway. Dylan could, if he wanted, just turn around and return to London on their arrival. Now that he had recently retired, he could choose to stay or not. George coughed and said,

"You see, the thing is Dylan, I've not been entirely honest with you. It's not that I've deliberately lied, it's just that I wanted to get to know you better before I dropped these bombshells. I planned on telling you it all, but this terrible situation has forced my hand. "

Dylan shook his head. As much as he wanted to scream, he maintained his cool exterior. After all, the man was going through enough already. While George's son had avoided serious injuries, his expectant wife wasn't as fortunate. Their fate still hung in the balance. "I might have known. I could tell that you were holding something back. I'm not stupid. What is it?"

George's leg tapped the train's side in rhythm to the clatter. "When I told you that Maria and I weren't great parents, I meant it. We put our own son on the streets when we found out he was gay. I called him all sorts of ugly names and washed my hands of him. He even tried to contact me at work and I was having none of it.

"At his funeral, I pretended to be there out of respect, wearing my doctor facade. I never got the chance to say how sorry I am. Maria and I cared more about living out the sham of a marriage and what the neighbours thought. Deep down, I'm a disgrace. But at least now you know."

Dylan reached over and placed his hand on his pasty friend. Yes, he was shocked, yes George and Maria had been monsters and yes, he wished he'd known before leaving. But how would an outburst help with the situation? George was already broken, and he didn't want to drive the final nail into his coffin. He said,

"This information isn't exactly an easy pill to swallow, but I understand. If you could do a similar thing to me, then I guess it was just as easy to do it to your son. Times were very different back then, weren't they? I imagine you lived in the shadows."

George tried to hold down a gulp of sludge but discreetly coughed it into a tissue. "Yes, I did Dylan. But Maria even stood by me when I got picked up for cottaging. Oh, and just to add insult to injury, she thinks you fled to London because of her?"

"Well, I did in a way. What do you mean?"

George leaned a little closer over the Formica tabletop that was separating them. Their conversation was already attracting the interest of a rather stout brown-haired man from across the aisle. "She thinks you left because you were in love with *her* and couldn't cope with seeing us together."

Dylan didn't know whether to laugh or cry. Well, the bloody hell fire. And the Oscar for best plot twist goes to, *drum roll please,* George Taylor. Was there nothing that this man wasn't capable of? "Well, George, you certainly know how to spin a good lie. That's a skill in its self. Just tell me, if it wasn't for all of this with your son- and daughter-in-law, would I have ever known?"

Without even giving it a second thought, George straightened up his torso and said,

"Absolutely. I just didn't want to scare you off straight away. I meant it when I said no more lies. I just wanted to get to know you again first. I've moved halfway across the country to find you. I wasn't going to blow my chances right away. "

They travelled in silence for the rest of the journey. It was only the train's reluctant arrival screech at the station that prompted Dylan to clear the air. "Just before we get off the train, I want you to know that I will do the right thing and stand by you. I get it, George. I really do. You're the most complex man that I've ever met. But tonight isn't about you, me, or even Maria, is it?"

And with that, the men jumped off the train and into the back of a taxi. Within ten minutes, they were outside the towering maternity hospital. This seven-storey, or eight, if you counted the delivery suite in the basement, was a shrine to maternity services within the nineteen sixties. And as much as George hated this concrete battery hen shed, it was not the time or place to discuss the finer points of British architecture. A stainless steel lift flirted them to the top floor. Two midwives in battle grey uniforms and cooky cutter black buns stood gossiping about some junior doctor at the other end of the lift. From what George could make out over the rumble of the shaft, the junior had been a bit of a heartbreaker with the student midwives. Dylan's eyes twinkled at George for the first time since leaving London. It was reassuring to hear that the hospital grapevine was as strong as it had been in their own junior doctor heyday.

There are some combinations in life that should never happen. And as Maria fiddled with her mohair blue cardy on entering the room, she'd found one. Some planners in the nineteen sixties must've got horribly drunk one night and thought they were trendsetters.

She stared in disbelief at a three-foot-long pine trough under the floor-to-ceiling waiting room window. It contained an assortment of plastic yuccas, cheese plants, and trailing shiny ivy. And just to make things worse, as if it was humanly possible, some bright spark had dressed the trough with a layer of grey pea gravel. The whole spectacle looked more like Tarzan's grave rather than a place to rest and reflect. She winced and lowered herself onto the horrible PVC modular seating units. That was typical of the NHS to spend all of its budget on a pile of worthless tat rather than suitable seating for a sixty-something-year-old bottom. She sidled up to her son, who was distracted by scraping thirty years' worth of dust from a cheese plant leaf. Damn it. He winced as she tried to put her arm around him. In the heat of the moment, she'd forgotten that he was still black and blue. Now content with his handiwork, he turned and faced her. This was no mean feat on these stupid seats, with or without lacerations. "Thank god you're here Mum. They've rushed Carla and Jack Junior to the operating theatre. The team is brilliant. They're doing everything they can to save them both, but it's touch and go. They're performing an emergency C-section. That's all I know."

Maria could see the look of fear in her son's eyes and desperately wanted to take it away. "I'm glad to be here, son. Your Dad won't be long. He's somewhere in the hospital. His friend Dylan has travelled with him for moral support."

A knock at the door interrupted them. A young midwife with blonde wispy hair hanging over a kind face said,

"Mr Taylor, your father's here. He's got a friend with him. Can I let them both in?"

"Of course, but thank you for checking first." Christian watched his mother in the corner of his eye wipe her hands on her pair of blue slacks, push her black bob over her ears and straighten up her cardy.

And then the door swung open as George entered. Dylan instinctively hung back a few steps behind to give the family space to make sense of each other. George did his best to hold back his tears, but it was pointless. Once he'd started, he just couldn't stop. "I'm so sorry, I'm so sorry. I promised myself that I'd keep it together. But seeing you and everything-"

"-Don't worry Dad. It hits us all in different ways. I'm just glad that you're here," Christian said.

All attention turned to the man looming behind George. Not forgetting his manners, Christian smiled and said,

"It's great to meet you, sir. Thank you for keeping my dad company on the journey. He's mentioned you on the phone before. I understand that you're a doctor too?"

Dylan smiled at the young man standing in front of him with an outstretched hand. He looked so much like his father. He gripped Dylan's hand gently. "It's my pleasure. I was a doctor, but I have just retired from the rat race. Please call me Dylan. When your dad told me what was going on up here, then of course I wanted to come and see if I could help. I didn't want him travelling alone. We were medical students at the City Infirmary together, but that was a very long time ago. George tells me you are in the family firm now."

"Yes, I am. I'm a junior doctor, currently doing a stint in oncology. My Dad is a hard act to follow though. I tell the staff that I'm just a learner, but they keep on comparing me to Dr Taylor Senior."

"Well, good to hear that. We all have to start somewhere, don't we, George?"

Maria's appearance distracted George. If anything, she looked younger, not older. It seemed as if a weight had been lifted from her slender shoulders. He blinked. "Oh yes, we all have to start somewhere, don't we?"

Christian was pleased to see his mother and father in the same room again. From the corner of his eye, he watched them coyly smiling at each other. He'd never seen this warmth between them before. Right, there was no time like the present for a quick stretch as his parents got re-acquainted. "I'm just going to the midwife's station for a progress report. Then I'll find a phone box and call Max. He's no idea what has been going on. I think I saw a phone at the ward doors so I won't be far away if I am needed urgently. If I sit in this pressure cooker for much longer, then I think I'll go mad."

George looked up at his son and smiled. "Right you are. We'll hold the fort here for a while. I'll come and get you if anything changes."

And then there were three. George was Mother and poured them all a plastic cup of water from the cooler. If their lips weren't dry, then his certainly were. His blue eyes radiated at Maria in a way that they hadn't since those days of heavy petting in the fuchsia-filled flower beds at Queens Park. But that was as ancient as the statue of Queen Victoria, who had presided over their pubescent fumbling. Even on their wedding day, he didn't look at her in this way. Breaking the silence, she waved the drink at him. "Thank you, George. I'm so glad that you're both here. There's been a lot of water under the bridge since we have all been together."

George didn't know what to say. Stuff it, honesty was the best policy. Well, that's what he was learning, anyway. "Thank you, Maria, you're right; there certainly has been. You look absolutely fantastic by the way. I've not seen you look this good in years. I'm pleased that we've been able to patch up our relationship. If nothing else, it's easier for the kids if we're getting on. To be honest I've missed you. And while I'm at it, I want to make one last confession before Christian comes back. I owe you that."

Maria felt the hairs on the back of her neck stand up. She clenched her ribs, ready to take the impact of George's blow once again. "What is it, George? Haven't you done enough already?"

"Yes I have, and I'm truly sorry for everything. I was a terrible husband and an even worse father. Dylan already knows what I did. But Maria, remember that I told you he left because he was in love with you?" George watched a familiar flick of pain return to his ex-wife's face. Her eyes were as black as her hair.

"Good God, no, I'm one step ahead of you both. The penny has just dropped looking at the both of you sitting there. You were playing hide the sausage weren't you? It's no wonder that Jane and Dylan couldn't be any more than friends."

The two men sat in silence. They seemed far more interested in watching the swirling shades of brown in the cushion flooring than either denying or confirming her suspicions. Once she'd grabbed her head from her stomach and calmed her breathing she was in a better position to make a decision. Whilst it would be easier to live in the past and revel in the hurt and lies, this was not healthy for herself or indeed anyone in the family. And George hadn't needed to be honest with her, either. The men could've easily kept up their lies. And did it really make any difference to her life now? She took a deep breath and put her hand on George's trembling knee. She said,

"It's okay, George. Now that I've thought about it all, let's just move on. Just be happy, my darling. Things were so different back then. It must've been so difficult to live a lie for all of those years.

"I was just caught in the middle of the past that wouldn't let people be openly gay. It was a criminal offence back then wasn't it? And how could two junior doctors show their love for each other at the City Infirmary without getting thrown out? From what Christian has implied, it's not all that much different now in certain teams. "

George couldn't have loved his Maria any more if he had tried. And yes, she was still his Maria, but not in the same way. For the first time, truth, honesty and understanding connected them. What was up with him? His cheeks were soggy all over again. "Thank you Maria, I just wish we could've been like this when we were married".

She chuckled and wiped his tears away with the edge of a tissue. "It just wasn't our time, darling. But that doesn't mean that I don't love you."

George kissed her on the forehead and tasted her familiar foundation on his lips. "And I love you too, Maria. I always will."

Dylan had been purposely quiet. The last thing he wanted to do was to ruin any reconciliation. It was getting hot in this stuffy waiting room. He unbuttoned his woollen bottle green jacket and took it off. Phew, that was better. Maria was totally right. There was no point in raking over the coals again. She'd every right to be angry, but had found the strength to forgive George. It was time to follow her lead. Dylan cleared his throat and said,

"George, I've been angry with you for far too long too. You've probably felt this over those fancy coffees. I've been conveniently hiding my anger behind Ali's death. I'm truly sorry. You see, I've never forgiven you for breaking my heart. Well, that is, until now."

George was off again. Where was his stiff upper lip when he needed it most? He'd been given a second chance. And if he lived to be one hundred, he wasn't going to waste this opportunity. "I don't know what to say to you both. It's true what they say isn't it? God appears in the most desperate of places. Thank you for everything."

The door swung open. Christian said, "Is everything alright in here Chaps?"

"They are now, son. Have you had any updates?"

He shook his head and sighed. "No, not yet. Carla is still in the operating theatre. I've phoned Max though. He wanted to come up straight away, but I told him to stay home till the morning at least. There's no point in us all being exhausted. Anyway, he needs to keep an eye on Wayne. It's still early days since his stroke.

"Max told me he would phone either Danni or his Aunt Bren first thing in the morning. One of them will sit with Wayne. And to be honest, as much as I love them all, I don't want any more people hanging around this evening. It's nice to just have the four of us."

Seconds turned into minutes and minutes into hours, but each one of them was no less painful in the wait to find out the fate of Carla and Jack Junior. There was only so much vending machine coffee and small talk that any of them could stomach. A knock on the security glass rattled in the news that they'd been waiting for. An outstretched hand and perhaps the biggest smile that Christian had ever seen bounced in.

"Good evening everyone. My name is Mrs Afolabi, and I'm the on-call consultant obstetrician. Let me just get to the point. Congratulations Mr Taylor. You're the father of a beautiful baby boy. That one is certainly a fighter. Although your wife has lost a lot of blood, they're both doing well.

We'll be monitoring your son in the special care baby unit for a while. But so far, so good. Congratulations again. Your wife is asking for you. Come with me."

This was one of those moments when words weren't enough. Maria, George and Dylan found themselves in a group hug. Christian then catapulted out of the door and to his wife and baby. He hadn't seen anything more beautiful in his life. He couldn't see the drips and drains, hear the beat of the heart monitors or smell the antiseptic lotion or blood. No, all of this faded away when he saw Carla. Tears dripped down his face as he kissed her forehead. He was the luckiest man alive.

She raised her head off the pillow. "Christian, is that you? I've been asking for you."

He gently stroked the hair out of her eyes. "Carla, I love you so much. You're my entire world. I thought I was going to lose you. Just don't move too much. Let me help you. You must be sore."

And then he saw the second most beautiful person who he had ever seen in his life. The same blonde-haired midwife who'd been checking on him all evening handed him his future wrapped in a white NHS blanket. Jack Junior was perfect. He instinctively gripped hold of his dad's little finger and gurgled. Christian cradled him close to his heart. And that is exactly where Jack Junior would stay until Christian would take his last breath. He had fallen in love with Jack long before he was born, but seeing his perfect son was priceless. In that tender moment, Christian knew exactly what the purpose of his life was.

# Chapter Fourteen

I was so eager to get to the hospital, but Wayne came first. It was kind of Danni to step in, especially as I knew she would be desperate to see our motley crew with the new arrival. I sat poised at the kitchen table and waited for her parrots to fly in my direction. Once pleasantries were over, I left the two of them chatting. In all the years she'd known him, this was one of the rare times they'd been alone.

He could easily picture Danni running a ward, teaching a group of students, or even a whole university, but he never quite understood why she'd became a nurse in the first place. He looked at her, smiled and said,

"Danni, can I ask you a question?"

Well, it hadn't taken him long to drop his poor innocent me routine and get to the nitty-gritty. Max was hardly through the door before he'd started the interrogation. "Go on then, seeing as it's you, what's going on in that pretty head of yours?"

Wayne offered her one of her favourite chocolate bourbons and went for it. "I've wondered what drew you to the lamp. I've never quite fathomed it out. Take it as a compliment, but you're the most unlikely nurse that I've ever met. You're hard as nails."

Damn it, that soggy biscuit had collapsed in her drink. There was nothing worse than sweet tea. She laughed to herself at the thought of Wayne trying to psychoanalyse her of all people. She Her nostrils flared as she said,

"Am I really *hard as nails,* Wayne? I've always been a, what does Malc call it, yes, an *independent headstrong woman*. He's just being polite. I know what I am. But I've had to toughen up. Sadly, I've learnt that in the world of nursing, if you're not at the table, then you're on the menu. It's dog eat dog and the higher you go, the worse it gets. Carla is exactly the same. We always have an opinion about everything, haven't you noticed? We're cut from the same cloth. To survive the smiling vipers, you just have to be hard-faced.

"But to answer your question, I wanted to become a nurse from an early age. When only knee height to a grasshopper, I spent hours playing hospitals with my granddad on the hearth until he got to the stage where we couldn't. He was my world. Sadly, we lost him to dementia. But he gave me a valuable lesson. He taught me to care with compassion. It's as simple as that.

"When I was a student nurse, I saw all sorts of things that I didn't like. Back in the day, the nurses were more interested in ritual and routine than putting the patient in the centre and working out from there. I hated it. In my nursing career, I've made it my mission to cut through such crap. But unlike many of the senior nurses in the snake pit, I haven't lost hold of my core values. These have served me well over the years."

"Right, I understand. That takes bravery and determination. As I said, I admire you, it's not an insult. You've always sorted my Max out." Wayne smiled at Danni as she rustled through the assortment of biscuits and poured herself a fresh cuppa.

"I'm not sure what Max has told you and what he hasn't. But he was in a pretty bad way before he met you. I've made it my mission to help him because I really can't stand how people treated him. Some of my colleagues at the City Infirmary carved him up and left him for dead.

"They were merciless bitches. He's not as strong as Carla and me. But that's not his fault. Sadly, he's a product of systematic abuse. If you pin him down and challenge him, he'll crumble. I've seen it happen. This is why I think he's drawn to strong women. Just look at Bren. No one is messing with her. She can give me a run for my money. Damit, I hope I haven't said too much."

Wayne gripped hold of her hand. "No, Danni, I know everything. It's OK. Whilst I wasn't around, I certainly heard Max's name being thrown around at the hospital. And let's put it this way; the staff weren't scattering confetti. He hurts deeply and takes things so personally. I've tried to smooth this out, but he's so sensitive behind those blue eyes. But equally, it's his strength. He always tries to see the good in people even when they've hurt him.

"I've not said anything to him, but when I was in hospital, I heard a few of his so-called 'neuro family' gossiping. They forgot that my side room was just behind the nursing station. These bitches couldn't understand how someone like him had done so well for himself. And just to make things worse, they said I was faking my stroke for attention. Once they found out about my mental health history, that was it.

"Apparently, I was 'functional', which is a nice way of saying that it was all in my head. I was almost relieved when they found the hole in my heart as it wiped the smile off those bitches' faces. In their next breath, the same nurses, and I use that term loosely, would then slap a smile on their face, come into my side room and pretend that they actually gave a fuck.

"Sorry for swearing. It makes me so mad. These are people who came to our home. I even delivered pizza for them when Max was on night shifts. One day, I heard Sister Sue rip them to shreds at the nursing station when she got wind of what they were saying. Bless her, she was the only decent one out of them.

"If I tell Max, it'll destroy him. He thought they didn't give a shit about his history with Daniel, but he's so wrong. But enough of my ranting, I'm sorry. Now whilst I top up the pot with fresh water, can I ask you something else, please?"

Danni ran her hand through her feathered spikes. What did Wayne want now? She watched him steady himself up on the table and grab his stick. Bloody hell, Pongo, move out of the way before you knock him over. He seemed to understand and gently slumped out of his path. After refilling the pot, Wayne pushed a trolley with hot drinks and even more biscuits to the table. At this rate, she wouldn't be able to get into her dark jeans and pink plaid blouse for much longer. And they called it middle-age spread. It was more like middle age contentment. "I'm so sorry that you went through that Wayne. Wait till I see Sharron Varley. But anyway, what is it you want to know now? This isn't mastermind and we're not playing the quick-fire round. "

Wayne plucked up the courage to ask the question that everyone had been thinking. Well, in for a penny, in for a pound. "I hope you don't mind me sticking my beak in, but how are things going with Malc? You seem much more chilled these days, that's all."

"No, I don't mind you asking. You're right, I'm happy. He's a diamond. I never thought that I'd go for anyone like him. You see, for years, I was the 'other woman' to an absolute arsehole. We carried on in secret. Not even Max or Jack at the time knew what was going on. But I'm over all of that rubbish now. Malc is my light in the storm. He's blinking hilarious with it too. For our first date, he took me line dancing and then onto a greasy spoon. But I loved it. He's not a complicated man. It's a case of what you see is what you get. And I like what I see."

Wayne felt a warmth that wasn't being generated from the hot tea. "Well, that one sounds like a keeper to me, Danni. If I were you, I'd marry him quickly before he gets away."

"You're not the only one to tell me that. Bren said exactly the same thing. And any-way, he's got to ask me first."

"Ask you? We're not living in the dark ages and you're not normally backward at coming forward."

And at that point Wayne quit while he was winning. The last thing he needed was for storm Danni to blow in again.

---

It'd been a long time since my feet had been over the threshold of maternity services. Seeing Danni and Jack Junior was more important to me than worrying about being recognised from my Daniel days. Even so, the hospec smelling lift floor was far more interesting than engaging in idle gossip with the midwifery staff. Hopefully, they wouldn't recognise me, camouflaged by a large blue rabbit. A rather stout midwife ushered me into the relative's room with strict instructions to wait. And that reminded me of that terrible but aptly true joke; *'What is the difference between a midwife and a terrorist.....you can negotiate with a terrorist.'* When I thought about it, I hadn't seen Mr and Mrs Taylor since Christian and Carla's wedding. They both looked up at me and smiled as the soft toy bounced past them and onto the seat opposite. All sorts of emotions sideswiped me when we made eye contact. But this wasn't the time or certainly the place for a re-enactment of 'Who killed J. R?' Instead, I took a deep breath and lied. "Hello there, please forgive my surprise, Mrs Taylor. I didn't recognise you for a second. You look so well. And Mr Taylor, it's great to see you again. Christian tells me you are living in London now. I hope you don't mind me popping up. I won't be long. I'm just desperate to see mother and baby."

Mrs Taylor grabbed my hand and gently shook it. "Not at all Max. It's lovely to see you. Please call us George and Maria. Carla has been asking after you. I know that you have met George before, but let me introduce you to Dylan. He's an old friend of the family."

I looked over to see a tall man, in his sixties, with salt and pepper cropped hair as he flashed his teeth at me. In his heyday, he must have been quite a looker in a 'Mr Darcy' kind of way. I could smell expensive aftershave as he leaned over the table. He thrust a designer gold watch, covering his large wrist, towards me. He said,

"Good day, Max. It is lovely to make your acquaintance. George has told me you have quite a merry band between you all. I understand you work with Carla at a local hospital. Is that right?"

"Yes, I do Dylan. Carla met Christian in my ward. That seems a long time ago now. They had their first date at Queen's Park and then toddled up to our house shortly afterwards. Right, I'm just going to check with the battle grey-clad mafia to see if I can nip in for ten. It was lovely meeting you."

Although completely washed out, I'd never seen Carla looking so happy. And when she passed me Jack Junior to hold, I could see why. He was the image of his dad and uncle. He smelt so fresh, so new, and so clean. I peered down at this bundle of innocence. His tiny soft white baby grow and matching hat had silver Mickey and Minnie Mouse embroidered into them. "Hello, my beautiful tiny tin soldier. I'm going to do everything in my power to make you happy, my baby Jack -in- a box. Your Uncle Jack wouldn't have it any other way." I didn't want to give him back. And at that precise moment, something had changed. I wanted a child of my own and that was that. But sometimes in life, you get what you need and not what you want.

Carla may have had a baby, but she hadn't pushed her brain out too. She was as perceptive as ever. "Max, he's beautiful, isn't he? Christian and I have been talking. We would be honoured if you and Wayne agree to become Jack Junior's godparents. What do you think?"

"Oh Carla, are you sure? I know Wayne will be ecstatic without even asking. I can't wait to tell him. Thank you, Carla. You have no idea how much this means to me. It's the closest we'll ever be to becoming fathers." I carefully placed Jack Junior into his plastic fishbowl and leaned in to hug her.

She winced as she tried to sit a little more upright. "Yes, we're sure Max. You'll be fantastic godparents. How's Wayne doing, anyway?"

"He's going from strength to strength. Danni is with him at the moment, so god knows what's happening back home. He's probably murdered her by now," I smirked. "You know how it is with these strong women. They always have to have the last word. Thanks for asking about him though. That's so thoughtful, especially after everything that you've just been through. I promised the midwives that I wouldn't stay long and tire you out. So I'd better go before they lynch me. I'll leave Bugs Bunny here on the end of the bed for company." And with that, I kissed them both and reluctantly left.

Now was as good as any time to introduce Len to the family mix. George had turned up with Dylan and had set the president already. But what should she wear? She could decide all of that after getting some sleep and taking a shower. But Maria wouldn't have missed any of it for the world. It was worth pulling an all-nighter just to see Christian's face when he realised he was a dad and Carla was stable. Some things in life are priceless, and this was one of them. She sat in her dressing gown on her favourite spot on her balcony and nibbled on a slice of granary toast. It was the only thing that she could stomach after all the previous night's excitement.

There was something decadent in waking up later in the morning and watching the whole rat race on the high street. Her mind wandered to the bank where she'd held court for more years than she cared to remember. But it was safe in her prodigy's hands now. And from what she'd heard on the grapevine, Von was doing a much better job as the bank manager than she'd ever done. The staff were happy and business was booming. Rumour had it that Von had even wiped out the staff's extra-curricular activities in the basement as well. Maria casually ran her hand through a potted fuchsia bush and watched the world go by. Goodness me, was that the time? Len would be here soon. It'd only seemed like five minutes since he'd dropped her off earlier that morning. She flung open her wardrobe door and tinkled at the top of the rails before quickly belting out a floral print dress, black cardigan, and matching shoes. Len knocked at the door as she was still putting the finishing touches to her face.

"You look wonderful, Maria. I can't tell that you've been up all night. You are quite the glamorous granny. Before we go, is there anything that I need to know?"

She curtsied like an extra in 'Gone with the Wind' and then giggled. "You daft bat, less of the granny and more of the glamourous if you don't mind kind sir. Joking apart, there is something that I need to tell you before we bump into my ex at the hospital. Well, er, the thing is, he's gay and has brought his *special friend* here for moral support.

They had a fling before he married me. We've already talked it through. I'm at peace with it all. I just wanted to put you in the picture in case someone brings it up."

"As long as you're OK, then it's fine with me. I'm here if you want to chat at any point." Len put his hand around her shoulder and placed a kiss on her cheek. Before they knew where they were, his car had arrived at the maternity hospital.

I just couldn't keep away. I nearly snapped Aunt Bren's hand off when she offered to come over and entertain Wayne. George and Dylan were sitting cosily together as I entered the visitors' room. It felt like I was plonking myself down between them in the back row of the movies. They now both smelt of the same expensive, tangy aftershave. I imagined that in all the kerfuffle George had simply forgotten to pack his. Luckily, Maria was hot on my heels. I slid up the seating to make room for her and the man she was linking. Maria and this stranger now sat opposite George and Dylan. She shuffled on the seating and watched George raise his eyebrows. There was no rush; she took a moment before introducing her prize bull. Eventually, she said,

"It's good to see you all, gentleman. May I introduce you to Len. He's my partner. We've been seeing each other now for quite some time. It's funny when I think of how we met. Len is the security officer in my complex of apartments. I think he just got sick of letting me out through the door with that stupid swipe thingy. In the end, it was easier to take me out on a date."

I watched George size up this greying broad man who sat opposite him in a denim shirt and cream slacks. And then he said,

"It's a pleasure to meet you, Len. It's lovely to see that you're both together. Can I please introduce you to Dylan? He dropped everything at the last minute to support me."

Len smiled and offered his hand to the two men. "Hello Dylan, good to meet you as well. It was nice of you to come up. Are you staying near here?"

Dylan turned his head slightly and flashed his eyes at George. "Oh, yes, we have booked into a charming hotel near to the hospital Len. I think you can rent the rooms by the hour if you understand what I am saying. The bed creaked like a rusty old gate last night. It was more of a see-saw than somewhere to rest."

I looked over at Maria and gestured my head towards Len. Luckily, she picked up on my less-than-subtle hint. "Oh, I'm sorry, Max, You don't know Len either, do you? A thousand apologies. My brain has got swept up in all of this baby business. I'm forgetting my manners. Len, may I introduce you to Max. Max, Carla and Christian are good friends. Carla works at the Eastfield with Max in older persons' care. I believe that they have known each other for years."

I looked at Len and felt almost sorry for him. After all, he'd been thrown into this Jane Austen novel without so much as a fan to hide behind. But he seemed happy enough to be hanging off Maria's arm. "Well, it's great to meet you Len. Yes, I'm a ward manager at the Eastfield. "

Len smiled from ear to ear. "Oh, the Eastfield, what a small world it is. I know the hospital well. The staff are so friendly. I was a maintenance man at the main site. It was always a pleasure to go over to that lovely little hospital. So you're the famous Max then. My son thinks the world of you. You gave him a job on your ward. His name is Billy."

"Billy, did you say?" I tried to regulate my breathing whilst playing my best poker face. Len wasn't the only one who needed a fan to hide behind now. In my head, I knew I needed to have a conversation with a certain healthcare assistant when I got back to work.

Len looked a little confused and said, "Yes, Billy, you must know him. He has long blonde hair and a bit of a lady's man. I'm sure he thinks he is some kind of rock god. I didn't even know that he was courting, let alone married until he phoned me. I'm still to meet his wife, Julie."

I smiled and thought of Laura. But it wasn't my place to connect the dots for either of them. Luckily, Christian appeared in the nick of time from behind the security glass in the door. Before I had the chance to reply to Len, we were mercifully diverted into all things Carla and Jack Junior. I left for my quick fix with Carla and Jack Junior whilst Maria was introducing her eldest son to her partner. Carla looked like she was the cat who had the cream as she snuggled Jack Junior into her breast. There was a part of me deep down that was jealous. But God made me gay for a reason and if I wasn't supposed to have children, then there was nothing I could do about it. They both smelt as fresh as a daisy. She looked up, smiled and said,

"Hello duck, it's great to see a friendly face. Christian has already warned me that Maria and her partner are visiting. I'll be on my best behaviour and try not to put my foot in it. His dad is still lurking about too. Is there a man with him?"

"As you well know, I'm not one for gossip. But looking at the pair of them, I'm convinced that they're more than just friends. They even smell the same. Now don't bust your stitches, but I've also found out that Maria is dating Laura's dad. You know, Laura from work. It was really awkward because he didn't know about her transition. And I certainly wasn't going to break the news." There was a part of me that wished I hadn't told Carla any of this, but equally, she needed to be kept in the picture. She had enough on her plate already and I didn't want any of it to slip out of her mouth by mistake.

"I'm glad that you have popped in Max, I am. I have 'baby head' and as you know, I'm not known for my tact. The last thing I need now is another family drama. I've got enough with Jack Junior to contend with." She looked down at her bundle of joy, who was contently gurgling in her bosom.

Phew. Thank God for that; we were both on the same page. "Well, that's exactly what I thought. Now I'd better go before Aunt Bren seizes up. She's sitting with Wayne. They all send their love and can't wait to see Jack Junior. Good night my darling, have fun, don't do anything that I wouldn't."

When I got back home, Wayne was trying to teach Aunt Bren to punch numbers and save them on her mobile phone. Although it was a bit like watching a scene from 'Educating Rita', our own Julie Walter's intentions were honourable. She figured that catapulting herself into the twenty-first century would mean that she could always contact someone whilst dog walking with Wayne. And when I thought about it, she was right. I just felt sorry for the poor man in the phone shop who must've developed a migraine shortly after Aunt Bren had left with her 'pay as you go' bundle.

# Chapter Fifteen

Despite being convinced that it was the right thing to do, I didn't want to upset the apple cart. Laura and I had worked together for the last three days, but I couldn't find the words. My staff had been nothing short of brilliant in supporting her transition. She was part of the Eastfield team and, like all good families; they stuck together. But what they didn't know wouldn't kill them either. Laura asked for her marriage to Julie to be kept quiet within the hospital fraternity. And I was more than happy to respect her wishes. Wayne's words rang in my head. "Max, be careful who you share your truth with. Not everybody needs to know everything about you." That advice was still as relevant today as it had been on the night when he turned up at my home and cooked me breakfast. I sat in my office, sipped a cup of strong tea, and tried to steady my left knee under the table.

Yes, of course, Wayne was right. But on the other hand, I didn't want Len to turn up on the ward and inadvertently cause a scene. I stared up at my office wall clock and sighed. There were around three-quarters of an hour left to speak to Laura before she left. In the words of Elvis, it was now or never. Luckily, as I stuck my head out of my office door, I caught her on the way back from the ladies' loo. My mouth was too dry to speak. All I managed was a quick tap on her shoulder. She sat in the chair, looking bemused and a bit irritated. Right, it was showtime. I said,

"Don't worry, you haven't done anything wrong. Now, I need to talk to you about something personal. But before I say it, I want you to know that it comes from a place of kindness and concern. Laura, you mean a lot to me."

"You're lovely. And although you've said nothing to me, the staff have told me you even did lots of trans awareness training with them before I returned. What's worrying you?"

I didn't want to pour any more oil on the fire. The young woman had been through enough already. Picking my words carefully, I said,

"This isn't easy for me to say. But here goes. I was at the maternity hospital the other night visiting Carla and Jack Junior. They are doing so well, by the way. Anyway, I bumped into your dad. He's dating Christian's mother. Her name is Maria. Once he found out that I was working as the ward manager here, he asked for you by your dead name. It wasn't my place to tell him. But equally, I don't want him finding out through idle gossip either. "

Laura grabbed hold of my hands. I passed her a tissue from my desk drawer. "Oh, my god Max. You really care about me don't you? I can see how upset you are. I've been meaning to talk to my dad. One thing at a time, as they say though. Julie and I needed to work out where we stood.

"I know he will ask about her. And to be honest, this won't come as a massive shock for him. I've always been a girl and deep down, he knows it. I used to dress in my mother's clothes until a lock appeared on their bedroom door. I heard them arguing about me regularly.

"This is probably why they split up. I can remember buying my first tennis skirt and top when I was about seventeen. He must've found it in my room and got rid of it. He didn't say a single word to me about it. Like everything in my childhood, we just brushed it under the rug and pretended it wasn't happening. Thank you, Max, I really mean it."

"I just want you to be happy, Laura, that's all." Thank goodness the cat was finally out of the bag.

---

Ouch. Hot mozzarella dribbled down Len's chin. He swigged another mouthful of wine to quench the heat. Well, that was his excuse, anyway. The salty crispness tasted great, but that never changed. But as much as he tried, he just wasn't hungry. His half-full glass reflected a distorted view of the world. Giovanni swung out of the kitchen to say hello and startled him back into the land of the living. Why on earth was he watching the convex candlelight when Maria was sitting opposite? And when he looked over and saw her watching him, he felt guilty. "Oh, I'm so sorry sweetheart, I was a million miles away."

Maria was concerned. Her Len was quiet tonight. What had she done wrong? Had she unknowingly upset him? Lately, she had been rather obsessed with Jack Junior, especially with Carla and the baby coming home this morning. She said,

"Are you OK Len? Sorry, have I offended you? I wouldn't hurt you for the world."

Good God, she thought it was her. He was such a miserable old toad. Without her, he'd be completely lost. "No, Maria, I'm the one who should apologise, not you. I've just been mulling over some news. Billy phoned me earlier. It was a difficult conversation."

"Why, he's not ill, is he?" Maria was worried now.

Len topped up their glasses and smiled. "No duck, he's not ill. He only told me something that I've known all of my life. He's now living as his authentic self. Both me and my ex-wife knew this deep down and argued for years about him. We hoped it was just a phase and he'd grow out of it."

This didn't make it any clearer in Maria's head. What was eating Len up so much that he couldn't finish his food? Trying to act cool, she said,

"What do you mean Len, did he tell you he was gay or something?"

Len shook his head. He couldn't find the right words. "Or something. And it's the '*or something*' bit that I am struggling with, even though, as I said, I knew. He told me he is living as 'Laura' now. He's always been a girl. "

It must have been catching. Maria was struggling to find the most appropriate reply. She swirled the wine around her glass and thought for a second before jumping in. "Len, I'm no one to judge. As you know, I was a terrible mother. There isn't a day that goes by when I don't regret what I did to Jack. I have his blood on my hands. Don't let that happen to Laura or you."

Len looked at this woman sitting opposite him completely differently. Yes, he knew she was attractive, but for the first time, he saw her genuine beauty. Maria was brave enough to bare her soul to him. And this, itself, was enough. It almost took him by surprise what fell out of his mouth next. But it felt right. "Maria, I love you."

What had he just said? Had he just told her he loved her? Oh shit, her cream blouse was completely ruined. The make-up would never come out. It had been a long time since anyone had said that to her, and even way back then, it was a lie. But this wasn't. It was real. And more to the point, the same thing bubbled up inside her. She grabbed his hands and leaned over the candle, almost setting herself on fire. "Len, I love you too. We'll get through this together."

I was rooting for Carla to get the job, but I knew I wasn't the right person to sit on the interview panel. She needed to be the next ward manager on her own merits and not because I was godfather to Jack Junior and had become as close as a brother to her over the last year. Luckily, Jan, Shirley and Eunice understood. But this didn't stop me from coaching her for the interview on the quiet. I looked at her and smirked before running through some likely scenarios. "Right, listen to me and remember these words. In your nursing career, you will see all sorts of practice. However, I will show you how to do things properly. These will be the tools in your nursing tool bag. Never drop your standards."

She burst into laughter. "You cheeky, bloody fool. But at least it's funny this time around."

Luckily, she took it well. "I'm sorry I couldn't help myself. I know it's a sick joke, but let's get down to business properly now."

In between playing with Jack Junior, I tried to help. I only had to look at him, and my heart melted. He chuckled just like his Uncle Jack. When his eyes twinkled, my heart stood still. And Wayne was just the same. We were both completely besotted. It was probably just as well that he had recovered from his stroke. It's hard to keep up with a two-year-old toddler who is into everything. Pongo was a constant source of entertainment. Jack climbed all over the poor dog. Even when he tried to pull his tail, our beautiful Labrador never reacted.

They were just two peas in the same pod. And to be honest, I'm not sure who was more interested in the jingly ball or activity centre.

Pongo loved nothing more than to push the buttons on the plastic sensory centre with his nose. He jumped in delight at the ringing and buzzing sounds it made. And it wasn't long until Jack Junior cottoned onto this. And as much as Pongo was boisterous with adults, he was always careful around his new playmate. It was lovely to see them snuggled up together on the sofa, fast asleep after a morning of play.

---

The first thing I noticed was a familiar song drifting from the day-room. *Ding Dong, the witch is dead! Which old witch? The wicked witch.* I wasn't expecting any of this. My plans for sloping off with no fuss had been well and truly scuppered. There was a four-foot-wide banner hanging from one side of the wall to the other. I suspected that this originally started life as a bedsheet. But they get ripped from time to time and do need replacing. Some kind soul had decorated the whole thing with 'Ding Dong, the Witch is Dead'. They had even sprinkled the dark writing with green glitter. Crepe streamers hung from the whole day room. Large pearlescent emerald and black balloons filled with helium shimmered at the centre of round tables covered with buffet food. I was mortally wounded and shook my head at the munchkins, who stood giggling around me. How dare they suggest I was a witch? *Ding Dong the wicked witch is dead, Wake up you sleepy head, rub your eyes, get out of bed.* Staff casually mingled with patients. Carla stood at the centre of the rabble in her new ward manager's navy blue uniform. It suited her so well. I wiped the tears from my eyes, threw my arm around her and shouted over the hilarity, "The thing is, you don't remember the film, do you? The Wicked Witch of the West was far worse than her sister. Good luck with Carla." *Ding-dong! The merry O- sing it high, sing it low. Let them know the wicked witch is dead.*

The room descended into a fit of giggles. It was lovely to see Jan, Eunice, Shirley, Laura and Danni having such a good time at my expense. But Carla stole the show. She pointed at the staff and mimicked the Wicked Witch of the West. In her best Margaret Hamilton voice, she said,

"I'll get you my pretties, and your little dog too. Don't make me release my flying monkeys."

Poppy tapped on a glass and cleared her throat. "Now, Max. It's no secret that I hated you when you started here. But don't get carried away with yourself, because as everyone knows, I generally hate all managers. But you've completely changed my mind. I don't want you to get too big-headed, but I've never been happier since you've been here. You're not a manager, Max. You're a leader and there is a big difference between the two. Although we will all miss you desperately, we send you off with our love."

I had gone. It was so difficult to speak through tears of happiness. "That's an absolutely beautiful thing to say, Poppy. You're so kind. You all mean the world to me. Bitter-sweet memories and all of that."

Carla appeared holding a long thin box covered in shiny green metallic paper. "We've had a bit of a whip round. Don't worry, it isn't a pair of slippers. I heard about that! We can't send you on to your job as a trainee advanced nurse practitioner without a goodbye gift, can we?"

I opened my present and found a beautiful top-of-the-range black stethoscope. It must've cost a small fortune. And just to finish me off properly, Wayne appeared from behind the door. "I suppose you were in on this then, too?"

He laughed and said, "What do I always tell you, babe?"

# Chapter Sixteen

Poppy had been watching for a while and didn't like what she saw. Whilst she was lovely for most of the time, her boss had an edge. The last thing Poppy wanted to do was to corner this lioness. But equally, Carla didn't scare her. No, Poppy was too long in the tooth for any such shenanigans and could certainly give as good as she got. If it wasn't such a sensitive subject, then she wouldn't be hovering at the ward manager's office with a dry mouth. The timing was everything. There was only half an hour to go before home time. Carla didn't raise her head from her desk. She said,

"Come on in Poppy and make yourself at home. I'm just going through the budget sheet. I'll be with you in a minute. Max warned me about this evil. I don't understand how these corporate drones get so excited over these numbers. They speak another language when I go to these stupid meetings about things that are far too removed from the bedside. If I hear them spout the words 'assurance, strategic plan or robust systems' once more, I'll scream! They need to get a bloody life. Why can't they just speak in plain English? "

Poppy sat quietly until her boss had finished venting her spleen about those cardboard corporate cut-outs. And at least that was something that they both agreed on. Poppy noticed a beautiful picture of Carla, Christian, and Jack Junior together in a silver frame. They looked like they'd fallen out of some glossy magazine. Carla sighed, rolled her shoulders, and threw the paperwork on her desk in disgust. She said,

"I'm sorry to keep you Poppy. It's my nemesis. I bet Max was glad to get rid of that. Anyway, what can I do you for?"

Poppy tried to buy a little time. "What a lovely photo of you all. How is Jack Junior doing? It only seems like five minutes since we were sending you on maternity leave."

Carla seemed a little calmer. She smiled as she glanced at the photo. "Oh, he's fine, thanks. He loves the nursery. I think it does kids good to socialise. Nanny Maria has him two days a week though. She spoils him rotten."

Poppy spied her moment now that Carla's head was back in the land of the living. "Oh, that's lovely to hear. That's what Nannies are for. Now Carla, I want to talk to you about something a bit personal. Well, it's more than a bit. And the thing is, I would rather you hear it from me because, If I have noticed, then I won't be the only one. This is coming from a place of kindness and concern so don't go off on one at me."

Her eyes were like saucers. "What is it? What have you done?"

Poppy shook her head and grabbed hold of her boss's hand. Trying to find the right words, she said,

"I haven't done anything. It's not me, this is about you. The thing is, people have noticed that you've stopped using the ladies' toilet on the ward. Staff have seen you running to the one upstairs in the main corridor. At first, I thought it had something to do with the fact that you wanted to get some fresh air or something. And then the penny dropped. It's no coincidence that all of this has happened since Laura has been using the ladies on the ward, is it? Are you struggling?"

Carla turned in her chair. She could feel her hackles rise. Good God, when had the toilet police moved in and made Poppy their chief?

It was a free country and she could pee, or otherwise, in any of the hospital toilets. But as much as she was ashamed to admit it, Poppy was bang on the money. Carla had a problem. She had bumped into Laura on one occasion over the paper towels. And that was enough. "No, Poppy, I'm not going to lie to you. You're very perceptive. I don't like Laura using the toilets. It makes me feel extremely uncomfortable. The ladies are for ladies and not for Laura. Whilst I am nice to her on the ward, I'm struggling with her whole transition thing. In my head, a girl is a girl, and a boy is a boy. I have no problem with people being gay though. That's different."

It took all of Poppy's strength to keep composed. "But Laura *is* a woman."

Carla felt her blood boil under her starched collar. "And I feel for her, I do. She has my every sympathy. I would probably march with her to support trans rights, but even then, there's a clear line in my head. I'll be kind and supportive on the ward. It comes with being a nurse. But it doesn't mean that I have to agree with everything. I'm paid to be impartial, so that's what I'll show.

"But *she's* not a woman Poppy. And you won't convince me otherwise. A woman is someone who menstruates. No matter how much oestrogen she takes or how much surgery she undergoes, she'll never be a woman. I just don't like sharing the ladies' toilets with her. That should be a place where I can relax."

Poppy shook her head and folded her arms. "Wow, Carla. Wow. Words fail me!"

"You don't need to say anything. I know well that my views aren't popular, but I can't help it. And I'm entitled to my opinion, it's called free speech. They'll probably be wanting a sanitary bin in the gent's next. And don't even start me on non-gender toilets. What will I do then? The world has gone mad. You did ask me, didn't you?"

"Yes, I did ask you, Carla. But that's the only thing that you're right about. You can't do this! You're supposed to set an example as the ward manager. The rest of the staff have taken it in their stride and welcomed Laura with open arms. But I guess Max did the legwork with that before he left. Laura hasn't had any problems with anyone. The team sees her as the woman that she is."

Carla smiled, but her eyes didn't follow suit. "Yes, thank you for reminding me I *am* the ward manager. I didn't know that. I know you mean well but just leave it alone, will you? Please close the door on your way out?"

Poppy flew to her feet. She was shaking. Carla was going to have it now. "Right then, we're playing that game are we? But no, I won't leave it alone. You've had your chance. I don't care if you are the queen of Sheba or Florence Nightingale herself. Wrong is wrong. You don't threaten me, you stupid woman. Who the hell do you think you are? I've chewed up and spat out more people like you than I've had hot dinners. Didn't Max warn you about me? When he started as the ward manager here we didn't exactly see eye to eye."

Carla glared at the red-haired woman wobbling underneath her spray-on staff nurse uniform. She stood up, put her hands on her hips and faced her staff nurse head-on. "Are you threatening me, Poppy?"

"No, definitely not. I'm just telling you how it is. When are you going to listen to reason? I thought you'd rather hear this from me. Shirley, Eunice or Jan won't stand for any of this here, lady. Now, you've got two choices. Either change your way or I'll take it to them. And then let's see how long that navy blue dress protects you. Grow up." Poppy turned and slammed the office door behind her before she said or did something that she couldn't take back.

The smell of garlic bread and fresh pasta drifted through the hall when Christian got in from a day in oncology. God, it was good to be home. He caught the back of Carla's red tee shirt and black jeans through the kitchen door. Even from behind, his wife looked stunning with her perked buttocks and long brown hair that danced towards her waist. She turned, smiled, put one finger over her lips and then looked at the ceiling. Was she wearing make-up? He casually ran one hand over her bum, kissed the small of her neck, and then turned to the dishes. Well, this was the very least he could do. Carla had been to work all day too. The oak kitchen table proudly sported a crisp white tablecloth, matching serviettes, and a bottle of plonk. Even a tea light in the central crackle glazed storm lamp was burning. This flickered an iridescent glow over their entire kitchen diner. Gloss white kitchen cabinets reflected the fragments of under-cupboard lighting. What had he done to deserve this? It wasn't his birthday and since having Jack Junior, meal times were more of a grab-and-go affair.

With the stainless steel extractor hood silenced and the gas hob now turned down to a low simmer, Carla said,

"Hello my gorgeous husband. It's been a while, hasn't it? Jack Junior is safely sleeping in his cot. I thought I'd surprise you. Neither of us are working tomorrow. There's a glass of wine over there with your name on it. Sit down and let me bring your food."

Christian didn't put up any resistance. As Carla dished their feast, he sat quietly with one ear on the baby monitor and his eyes on the most beautiful woman whom he had ever met. She was a fantastic wife and mother. He smiled to himself as he watched her unhook her hair from her hoop earrings. Pasta sauce and her curls just weren't a good combination. Within a few minutes, they were sitting opposite and staring into each other's eyes. "This is a lovely gesture, thank you. I'm so lucky to have you. "

Carla flashed a smile. "You know, things have been pretty rough lately haven't they? We don't seem to get a minute to ourselves. It's knackering isn't it?"

Christian sprang to his feet before he had the chance to reply. He quickly shoved a piece of garlic bread in his mouth before disappearing upstairs. Within a few minutes, he returned and said,

"Jack's fine, darling. I think he was just grumbling in his sleep. But yes, it's bloody hard work at times."

Carla sighed deeply and poured them both a top-up. "Thanks for going, duck. Can I talk to you for a minute before he starts again?"

Christian was worried. "Yes, of course. What's on your mind?"

"I've made a right tit of myself today at work. I'm lucky that they haven't sacked me, to be honest. I spoke to Poppy like she was something on the bottom of my shoe. Any other member of my team would've gone directly to Eunice or Shirley. I'm so angry with myself for losing it. She was only trying to help me. But when the red mist descended, I completely lost control."

Christian listened patiently as his wife opened up. It wasn't until hearing the entire story that he said,

"Carla, it's like this. I love you, but I won't sugarcoat it. We both know that my mother and father were no angels. And just look at what happened there. They thought they were doing the right thing too and wouldn't bend. Even if it cost the life of my brother. Don't let the same thing happen to Laura. I know that you're better than that."

She slapped her cutlery down on the table and stared at her husband. "Oh my God, you're right. And there was me condemning your parents for what they've done. I'm nothing but a bloody hypocrite.

Poppy was right. I'm not going to wait until Monday to sort this out. She's on duty tomorrow. Whilst your mum has Jack Junior in the morning and you're at your rugby practice, I'll nip up to the ward."

Christian grabbed her hand from across the table and kissed it. "And that's exactly what I love about you so much. You may be fierce, but you're not afraid to hold your hand up and say when you're wrong. Now pour me another glass of wine. Let's dance. "

The couple slowly swayed around their kitchen diner to the gentle hum of the baby monitor and the flickering storm lamp. It was perfect. Christian felt so good in her grip. His firm body was the perfect tonic for her shit of a day. And if he played his cards right later, she planned to rekindle a little more than just romance between them. Well, that is, if Jack Junior would let her. She still had a few tricks up her sleeve.

Carla was true to her word. She grabbed a bunch of flowers from the florist in town before heading to the Eastfield. She always made a point of picking out fresh flowers. Nothing expressed "I couldn't be really bothered, but here you are anyway," more than a wilting generic bouquet from the local supermarket. Luckily, Poppy was susceptible to the white rose and eucalyptus leaf display. "Poppy, I'm so sorry. I don't know what to say to be perfectly honest. I've been such a cow. There's no excuse for any of it. I've had to do some soul-searching, but yes, you are right, Laura is just as much a woman as you and me. I'm ashamed of the things that I said about her. I'm a work in progress, but will do everything I can to change. I also treated you terribly. It just tells me what a wonderful woman you are for not hanging my navy uniform out to dry. "

Poppy looked at the flowers that were sitting on the ward manager's desk. These weren't cheap supermarket crap. It had been a long time since anyone had bothered with her. At least Carla had attempted to say sorry properly. "We were both furious with each other. It's not entirely your fault. I shouldn't have threatened to report you. That was a low dig.

"You see, the thing is, I'll always open my mouth and protect my staff. Thank you for levelling with me. I'm here if you want to talk your feelings through. Just don't go off on one if things happen that make you feel uncomfortable. That mouth of yours will get you into a lot of trouble if you're not careful."

"I know I'm a rent a gob. But give me a chance and I'll prove to you I can change." And at that moment, Carla knew exactly who the next deputy ward manager should be.

# Chapter Seventeen

There were baptisms by fire and then there was Belle Reve Community Hospital. This red-bricked pile housed two wards, an outpatient therapy centre and an x-ray department. Just like the Eastfield, it too had served the needs of older people within the local community since Queen Victoria had sat on the throne. I had always been quietly impressed that a scattering of community hospitals cared for the unique needs of the local population. This meant that the patients were in familiar surroundings and within touching distance of their families and friends. Following a period of rehabilitation, many of the patients returned home. Ongoing care was based upon an assessment of the person's need and not whether they could afford it. Just as Nye Bevan had insisted when he spearheaded the NHS, this model was based upon his belief that, *Illness is neither an indulgence for which people have to pay for, nor an offence for which they should be penalised, but a misfortunate cost which should be shared by the community.* It's quite interesting that politicians who believe that funding the NHS is not a 'bottomless pit' are usually the same people who can afford to go private.

I pulled into the car park of the Belle Reve on my first morning, switched the engine off, unwound the window and took a minute to gather my thoughts. Despite endless amounts of fabric conditioner, my neck and chest were sore. The crispness of the new white tunic and burgundy epaulettes may have looked professional, but were like sandpaper around my delicate bits. And the black non-iron trousers were waxing my bikini line without even trying. I was just glad that my training hadn't started in the summer months or I would walk like the tin man on a bad day. But it was a price worth paying. I looked up at the hospital and gingerly got out of my car. As luck would have it, Belle Reve's experienced Advanced Nurse Practitioner was going on a secondment for twelve months. This left a gap to be filled by a starched trainee.

I itched through the revolving door and into the hospital. Leaves followed me into a damp central reception, which was framed by two large arched windows. In between them, a friendly-faced lady in a no-nonsense black trouser suit and white blouse sat at her pulpit, ready to funnel the congregation to the various departments. As I headed towards the reception, a familiar hospital smell comforted me. The clatter of a meal trolley passed me on its way to the wards. I could tell it was Monday from the unmistakable smell of cheese flan and beef hotpot. You could set your fob watch by the daily choices. Somehow, Fish Day Friday always made me feel sick. My thoughts were intercepted by a short red-haired matron wearing a purple tunic top. Shit. All sorts of soreness rose to the surface of my polycotton when I saw her. Jack was right, histamine doesn't lie. But sadly, nurses do. But did she recognise me? Although now considerably heavier in the foot, there was no mistaking it was her. This smiling blob held her hand out towards me. It took me all of my time to make eye contact and shake her hand. Back in the day, she worked as a staff nurse when I was a student nurse at the City Infirmary. But that was then, and this was now. Debbie might be my new boss, but she wasn't going to stop me. She needed me more than I needed her, even if I was a trainee.

I climbed the steep stairs behind her to the attic offices. When she reached the summit, she was exhausted. It was hard not to laugh. At one point, I thought I was going to have to push her up the narrow stairway. This labyrinth may have looked innocent enough, but as we navigated along the rows of dark oak doors, anyone who was anyone had an office along here. I passed several brass door plates which read, 'Hospital Matron,' 'Hospital Manager,' and 'Community Service Manager.' Just before reaching the "Advanced Nurse Practitioner Office' my eyes landed on a door with 'Community Matron' etched on the brass plate. Goodness me, my door was next to theirs. These high-profile nurses worked with the top ten percent of patients with complex health and social needs within their own homes. Their sole purpose in life was to assess, plan and prescribe under the umbrella of advanced nurse practice to alleviate the risk of preventable hospital admission. These highly skilled nurses could walk on water. They gained the reputation of being experienced practitioners who worked independently and autonomously. And now my new office was next door to such nursing royalty. I was equally star-struck and intimidated at the same time. Debbie swung open the door to my new world. It was nothing short of beautiful. The top of an arched stain-glass window offered fragmented hues of red, green and blue across the cream walls. Pam, the previous advanced nurse practitioner, had left a tidy ship. A sturdy mahogany corner desk was positioned under the window. It offered a breathtaking view of the tree-lined hospital entrance below. The latest computer sat proudly perched on a docking station. There were a series of heavy set shelves, almost bulging with medical and nursing textbooks. A small fridge buzzed in the corner of the room. On the top of the fridge, there was even a tree of gleaming white mugs. I noticed a card with my name on it by the kettle. Debbie smiled when I ripped open the envelope to see a blue background with

"Congratulations on your new job" embossed in gold writing upon it. I opened the card and found that the ward teams had signed it. There was a small basket of speciality tea and coffee wrapped in clear cellophane. This had a matching blue tag that simply said 'Welcome Max' written on it. And suddenly I felt guilty.

"The staff wanted to make you feel welcome, Max. If you look, Pam has signed it too and written her contact details down in case you need anything. Welcome to Belle Reve. It's our pleasure to have you here. Don't worry, the nursing staff are aware you're a trainee. They're a good bunch, though, and shouldn't give you any hassle. I've heard great things about you. Eunice and Shirley sing your praises. You're not going to let me down now, are you?"

"Thank you. What a lovely gesture. And yes, I'll do my best."

Her eyes twinkled as we sipped from the new mugs. And then she addressed the enormous elephant that was sitting in the room. "Max, I know what you're thinking. And you're right, I was an absolute 'c u next Tuesday' in my younger days. But let me try to make it up to you. I didn't stick up for you because I was too scared that those bloody nurses would start attacking me instead. You didn't deserve any of that crap."

That took a lot of bravery and if nothing else, she was honest. "Debbie, thanks for that. I appreciate that want to clear the air between us. Let's just draw a line under it now. It sounds odd, but I've taken a lot of comfort from Maya Angelou over the years. She's helped me to process it all. As she said, 'I am human and as a human, I can be equally capable of great kindness and great cruelty'. That has helped me to get my head around things. Those nurses were capable of both. "

"You're spot on Max. They weren't all bad or all good. And that includes me too. But I am sorry for putting you through that." Debbie looked as if she was about to cry.

"Let's just move on. Actions speak louder than words, don't they?" And with that, I changed the subject. I wanted to know all about the hospital; the staff, the facilities, the patients, and the list went on. Once she'd showed me around and introduced me to the teams, I relaxed. My first impression of the hospital was great. All the staff were friendly, chatty, and welcoming. But more to the point, my experienced eye told me they put the patient at the centre of everything. And that's all that mattered to me.

But on the second day, the kid gloves were well and truly taken off. The hospital paid two local General Practitioners from a local surgery to provide medical cover. They'd agreed to mentor me within the formal terms and responsibilities stipulated in this contract. A three-year master's program would assess me in every way humanly possible. Like Danni had said, this transition wasn't for the faint-hearted. I could regurgitate the theory, but couldn't put this into action. The four pillars of leadership, education, research, and advanced clinical skills form the foundation of advanced clinical practice. Eunice had done this for years without batting an eyelid in her role at the Eastfield. She was extremely experienced, but so unassuming about it all. Even though she appeared calm on the outside, she was highly skilled at coordinating clinical care in collaboration with patients, families, and caregivers. And now it was my turn to give it a go. Well, that is, once I had met with my mentors and worked out how to use my stethoscope.

The two doctors had been in the local community since god was a lad and what they didn't know about the area wasn't worth knowing. They had also held the contract at the Belle Reve for many years. But that didn't mean that they wanted to help me. I quickly learnt that this brother and sister team were more interested in getting in and out of the hospital as quickly as possible. Despite signing a lucrative contract to support me, they treated me as if I were an inconvenience. They'd been the same with my predecessor when I asked around. This didn't offer any consolation, unfortunately. I just never realised that the most important pillar of advanced clinical practice was learning to swim with the sharks if you didn't want to be ripped to pieces. The problem was, even though they were supposed to support my development, I was just chump. Thursday lunch time was the worst part of the week. I dreaded it so much to the point where I didn't sleep on a Wednesday night. In between their morning and afternoon surgery, one of them would conduct a whistle-stop ward round on each ward. They were making my life so unhappy, but I didn't want to rock the boat.

*I sit and wait, does an angel contemplate my fate? And do they know the places where we go when we're grey and old?* Before I knew what I was doing, I was slurring along to the words of this local lads' song, with tears running down my cheek. Danni had gone to help Wayne carry another round of drinks. I watched them giggle with Simon and Zuri at the bar. From what I could gather, she was trying to get the couple to resurrect their male review act. I heard her shout something about baby oil being on special offer at the chemist on the high street. Had the woman got no shame? *And do we know the places where we go when we're grey and old?* I felt Aunt Bren's bones slide up against me and her heavy perfume waft under my nose. Her new charm bracelet jangled against her empty glass in rhythm with Robbie's heartfelt voice. *Cause I have been told that salvation lets their wings unfold.* And then she picked up her glass and swigged the last dregs out of it before the next one arrived.

"I'm dry as a nun's chuff, Max. I wish they would hurry at the bar. Oh my goodness, you're crying. It's this bloody music, isn't it duck?

Robbie doesn't call it the funeral song for nothing. But don't be sad. Jack wouldn't want to see you in this state would he?"

Why did everybody automatically assume that I only cried if it was about Jack? He was having a ball in the afterlife. I imagined him leading Michael astray and getting up to all sorts of cloud-jumping chaos. And whilst I missed him, I was equally comforted to know that he was fine. But Aunt Bren meant well. The last thing I wanted to do was to upset the closest thing that I had to a mother. I gently grabbed hold of her hand and swayed towards her on the seat. "You're the one who is the Angel, my darling. I'd be lost without you. I'll never forget what you have done for me over the years. You've never turned your back on me. I love you, but I'm not crying over Jack for a change." *So when I'm lying in my bed, thoughts running through my head and I feel that love is dead.*

But she didn't get the chance to reply. Danni and Wayne were back from the bar and still giggling like two naughty school girls. *I'm loving angels instead.* Slapping down the drinks on the driftwood table top, Danni half heard the tail end of our conversation. She looked at me, picked up her pint, and blew the head off her beer at me. Sometimes, she was as blunt as a broken pencil. "What's up with you now? Can't we just have a few drinks for a change without it turning into some sort of melodrama? Believe it or not, the world doesn't revolve around you."

I was still trying to absorb what she'd just said to me. The heartless cow. And after everything we'd been through together. The bitch just couldn't stop herself from going for the jugular. But why? Now they were tears of anger. I saw Wayne in the corner of my eye shake his head from side to side. Aunt Bren threw mascaraed daggers at Danni but remained silent. She stiffened up against me. They both knew what was coming. "Why change the habit of a lifetime Danni? We've certainly heard enough of your crap here over the years too. Since how long have you been a saint? Just leave it alone for a change will you?"

She was stunned into submission. The worm had turned. "Max, you're right. I'm sorry. This mouth of mine will get me into a lot of trouble one of these days. I don't want to fight."

"I'm sorry too. I shouldn't have gone that far. Beer and heartache just don't mix. At least Carla knows when to rein her mouth in. We're just feral. I'm all over the place and can't sleep. It's these two doctors. They're trying to make my life hell. I just want to do my best. The course is hard enough without putting up with their crap. They shout at me in front of the staff and patients if I get things wrong.

"I'm not ungrateful, but I feel like jacking it all in. The other day, on the ward round, one of them threw a set of notes at me. He flung it so hard that it hit me in the stomach. And then he expected me to pick it up like a fucking lap dog. I can't do this. It's triggering all sorts of stuff in my head. I'm not prepared to go back there for love nor money. But everyone at the Belle Reve just takes it as the norm. Those two demons have been like it for years."

Danni took a filo fax out of her black handbag. She was struggling to turn the pages. Doing her best to make sense of her spider's crawl, she said,

"Just remember, I may be a bitch, but believe it or not, I'm *your* bitch. Let me see. Yes, I have a free couple of hours on Thursday at lunchtime. Now Max, instead of doing the ward round, I'd like you to go to your office and wait for me there. I think I need to remind these doctors that the University makes a sizable financial contribution to their contract. And if they don't want to mentor trainee advanced nurse practitioners, then I have a whole host of other doctors who do. It's as simple as that. Another practice within spitting distance would snatch my hands off. That surgery is full of young dynamic medics.

When I think about it, maybe it's time to review our contracts. I'll chat to Jan and Debbie."

Nobody messed with Danni or anyone that she loved and got away with it. What was the point of climbing the ranks if she couldn't protect her own? As she'd warned Wayne, that if you weren't at the nursing table, then you certainly would be on the menu. She smacked her lips, took a swig of beer and decided she was ravenous. *And through it all, she offers me protection, a lot of love and affection, whether I'm right or wrong.*

# Chapter Eighteen

I plodded up the concrete flight of steps from the carpark to the Belle Reve and contemplated my future. The metal handrail was freezing in my hand. Part of me wanted to turn around, get back in my car, and go home. But on the other hand, I knew it would take less than a day to replace me. Danni had told me that many nurses had applied for the trainee post. This translated as don't let me down as there is a cue of people waiting to jump into your shoes. But what if the sling backs just didn't fit me? What then? I dragged myself through the entrance doors, trudged up the narrow stairs, and finally reached my office.

Where had Debbie sprung from? Her words startled me. "Max, I thought I'd wait for you here until you showed up."

I collapsed onto the chair at my desk. "I'm sorry. I was in a land of my own. Let me get straight to the point. I can't believe what's been going on with those two doctors on my wards. Why didn't you come to me with it?"

I thought about all the things that I could've said. But none of them would make any difference. And there was no point in getting angry. Looked directly into her eyes, I said,

"I'm the new boy here, and as they say, mud sticks. So, I can't afford to cause any trouble. According to the staff, it seems like this has been going on here for years. No wonder Pam only stayed for a year. I used to think it was a case of 'shut up and put up,' but I can't do that anymore.

I've had enough of being screamed at. Are you seriously telling me you didn't know what the doctors are like? Sorry, but that's hard to believe."

"I just didn't realise that it was as bad as this."

"You sat there and told me how sorry you were about what happened to me as a student nurse. All the time you knew what was going on here right under your nose. You've actually had the nerve to say that you were sorry for not sticking up for me all of those years ago. The worst part is that I actually believed you. I'm so stupid. I guess a leopard can't change its spots and a whore doesn't change their knickers either. Which one are you?"

"Yes, you're right. I'm so sorry. I've already had my head bitten off about this. Jan and Danni didn't mince words."

"And so you should. I've been on the verge of packing all of this in. My nursing career hasn't exactly been plain sailing, as you know. Maybe I need a total career change. But then again, I wouldn't want to give you the satisfaction of getting rid of me so easily. Many have tried in the past and have come unstuck. And let me tell you something matron, you're certainly no different. I'm the grit in your teeth that just won't go away, no matter how much you bloody floss."

She sat shaking her head and snivelling. But I had seen a milder version of this pantomime when I first started. Although she couldn't make eye contact, she said,

"No, don't leave, Max. See this through. A couple of doctors from a new practice near here have already taken over. Just give it a go. See how you feel in a month. Danni has suggested that we arrange regular clinical supervision for you with someone you trust. Eunice has agreed to come over every week and spend an afternoon here. This hospital is very similar to the Eastfield. She'll support and mentor your development better than anyone I know.

And before I forget, you're right, I've been walking around with my eyes shut. You've got every right to be angry with me. "

What had I got myself into now? I'd only come to the Belle Reve for training and experience. But sometimes in life, you get what you need and not what you want. Debbie's card was well and truly marked. Eventually, I went to the wards. Joan was just coming out of her ward manager's office. It was hard to see where this stout woman in her fifties ended and her office began. She'd worked at the hospital for more years than she cared to remember. There was nothing she hadn't seen and done during her career. Instead of giving me her usual list of jobs, she beckoned me over. It was like getting an audience with the queen. She fumbled for her glasses, that hung on a chain around her neck. This was her way of showing me she was not only in the zone, but meant business. She huffed on the lenses and tried to clean them with a tissue. With the smears safely removed, she said,

"Well, young man, you've caused quite a stir for someone who has only been here for five minutes. Debbie's face was a picture when Jan and Danni had finished with her earlier. I was coming back from the ladies' loo and spotted her. Let me put it this way: you could've fried eggs on her forehead. It took me all of my time to stifle my snigger.

"Good for you. I've been trying to tell her to get rid of those two doctors for years, but she doesn't listen. You wouldn't believe the amount of arguments that I've had with our illustrious matron about the way these bullies have treated my staff. There's been many of an occasion when I've tackled the terrible duo myself. They thought they were Teflon-coated.

"Since Debbie has drafted young Sarah from the City Infirmary to run the ward opposite, she doesn't take a scrap of notice of me. It's sickening to watch the pair fawn over each other. Apparently, they worked at the mother-ship together. She thinks that I'm past it and

I know nothing. Debbie could certainly learn a thing or two from my grey locks, but she only sees the grey and not my experience.

"The other morning, she laughed at me in front of the entire staff because my hand was shaking. It took her less than five seconds to point out that my cuppa was dripping on my shoes. And she didn't ask me how I was. Spending the entire night awake with my Clive in the accident and emergency unit and then coming to work would make any-one shake. Luckily, it was only his hiatus hernia and not a heart attack this time. Even , I could still run rings around the pair of them if I wanted to. "

Bless her, Joan was a trooper. These unassuming angels form the backbone of the NHS and want nothing in return. Although I admired her dedication, there was a part of me that wondered why she'd kept quiet about this toxic culture for so long. Why hadn't she escalated it sooner? As she stood fiddling with the beaded string to her glasses, I clicked. Deep down, fear paralysed her. And how stupid of me for not recognising this. I, of all people, should've smelt that. Something made me gently place my hand on her shoulder. I said,

"I'm so sorry to hear about your Clive. Jan is really approachable and, without wanting to put words in her mouth, would bend over backwards to support you. There's all sorts of flexible working policies to help. Why don't you arrange a meeting with her? I'll come along for a bit of moral support if you'd like.

"And whilst I'm so pleased that you stick up for your team, you should never carry the burden alone. I'm here now and you can chat with me anytime. We must stand together and make our voice heard. If we don't have the freedom to speak up, then nothing changes. We'll hold these bullies to account; mark my words. But we'll do it calmly without compromising our own dignity. For me, it's all about the patients. Unhappy and unsupported staff lead to all sorts of problems."

She looked at my hand on her shoulder, smiled and tilted her head. Her cheek brushed back the back of my hand. Her voice lowered as she said,

"I knew I could talk to you and that you'd understand. I don't want to rub your nose in it, but I was working on the mother ship as a staff nurse when you were a student. Thank god Bren stepped in at the staff canteen and scooped you up. I was on my way over, but you'd left my then. Those bitches, eh? I saw how they treated you."

"Oh, yes!" A rogue tear ran down my face. "That's why we shouldn't tolerate this crap."

With a new friend under my belt, I headed towards the notes trolley and spotted a petite lady wearing a beautiful gold and blue sari thumbing through the files. She wouldn't have looked out of place as a leading lady in a Bollywood romance. She stopped, smiled and said,

"You must be Max. It's a pleasure to meet you. I'm Parvati. I'm one of the new doctors here. It's my first day, so I guess you'll be showing me the ropes."

"It's nice to meet you. I can't promise anything though. It's all new to me as well."

We spent the next few hours reviewing all the patients in Joan's ward before nipping over to do the same for Sarah. Parvati was nothing short of a miracle. I learned more in those four hours than I had in my entire time at the Belle Reve. And she didn't make me feel stupid for not knowing the answers either. She just calmly listened and gently guided me as we went from patient to patient. Her bedside manner was second to none. Suddenly, I felt a weight being lifted from my inexperienced shoulders. By the end of her ward round, we were chatting like two old friends.

"You'll be fine Max. Don't worry about a thing. Oh, by the way, Sam will be in tomorrow. We'll be doing opposite days. Just contact me at the surgery if you need anything in the meantime. Now, I must dash. I'll have a waiting room full of patients when I get back."

And Sam certainly *was* in the next day. I could smell him before I could see him. Tangy top, spicy middle and earthy bottom notes drifted towards me. I was no connoisseur of men's aftershave by any stretch of the imagination, but I could recognise expensive when I smelt it. All I knew was that he was fresh off the train from London and now working as a general practitioner in the local area. He bounded over like an excited Labrador puppy and thrust a muscular arm in my general direction. But instead of trying to shake my hand, he unexpectedly put his large shovel on my shoulder. Gosh, it was hot in these wards. I said,

"Hello, you must be Sam. Parvati told me it's your day to come. I'm Max."

His hand still lingered on my shoulder. "Well, howdy Max, the pleasure is all mine."

It was hard not to stare. "Yes, er, welcome to Belle Reve. I'm looking forward to working with you. Is that an American accent I can detect?"

"It sure is. I'm originally from the Sunshine State. But I've always been fascinated with you Brits. A job in London tempted me over the pond a few years ago. I then fell in love with you all and decided to stay. I trained as a general practitioner in London. And here I am, at the Belle Reve, footloose and fancy-free."

I watched him run his hand through his brown hair. As he moved, the fluorescent tube lights highlighted his blonde quiff. This Belle Reve's answer to Patrick Swayze looked so out of place in the hospital ward. I could see him in a swanky Hollywood restaurant or the set of a blockbuster movie, but definitely not at the other end of a notes trolley. After studying the patient's case histories, we reviewed a gentleman who'd been admitted that morning. Joan's nursing team was concerned about his behaviour. Sid had been transferred to the ward for assessment and rehabilitation. Previously, he was an inpatient at the City Infirmary. When his morning carers arrived at his bungalow, they found him on the floor in pain, lying in his own urine. It was unclear how long he had been there. Sid had been living with Alzheimer's dementia for over two years. All he knew was that he was cold, hurt, frightened, and stuck on an upturned rug. Unfortunately, he had fractured his left hip in the fall, possibly because of a urine infection. Before coming to Belle Reve, the medical team on the mother ship treated him with antibiotics and intravenous fluids for the infection. They also performed a left total hip replacement surgery and reviewed his medication to ensure he received regular pain relief. It turned out that Sid had difficulty taking his medication at home. Since coming to us, he couldn't settle.

The clinical situation wasn't out of the ordinary. Sid had a delirium superimposed onto a history of his known Alzheimer's dementia. Delirium is an acute, fluctuating a syndrome of disturbed consciousness, perception, attention, and cognition. It can also cause behavioural disturbance, personality changes, and psychosis. Sam and I agreed that Sid may have hyperactive delirium as he was presenting with inappropriate behaviour, hallucinations, and agitation. We knew Sid couldn't fully understand or remember our conversation with him. However, he recognised our presence when we knocked on his door and introduced ourselves. Upon entering the room, the eighty-five-year-old man took off his pyjamas, got on his bed, and lay on his front. He then raised his legs, exposing his anus. His skin hung loosely from his frail body like an old sheet. I glanced at Sam. He was trying his best to hide his upset too. This poor patient cocked his head in fear and said,

"No fucking please, no fucking today. No money. No fucking."

Whatever Sam and I were there to do didn't matter. If Sid needed to be examined, then Parvati could be called. Two female staff members comforted the traumatised man. The team immediately raised a safeguarding concern. Further investigations revealed Sid had been a sex worker most of his life. His nephew was in tears when he explained how Sid worked in the red-light district. He'd faced abuse and neglect throughout his life as a child, teenager, and adult. In his confused state, he was reliving his worst nightmares. Although I wanted to comfort him, it was the wrong thing to do.

"Shall we find somewhere quiet and chat?" Sam whispered into my ear when we came out of the side room, still shaking.

"That sounds great, thanks. I've an office upstairs. We won't get disturbed there."

It was really strange. Neither one of us spoke until safely tucked into my attic room. As I passed him his cappuccino, I accidentally brushed my arm against his on the way to my swivel desk chair. Either he didn't mind or he hadn't noticed. Now sitting within touching distance, I said,

"That was bloody awful. The poor man. It just goes to show that we've no idea about what really goes on in people's lives."

"You're right there Max. No one knows, do they? I wanna check in with you. Are you OK?".

"That's so lovely of you, Sam, thanks for your concern. It's just triggered me, that's all. How about you?"

Sam sipped his coffee and licked the froth from his top lip. He tilted his head and squeaked the plastic chair under him. "Well, I'd like to say that I'm a big boy and I'm fine. But it real shocked me too. It sure was a terrible situation. I'm not gonna lie, that poor gent pushed my buttons. I've only been at the practice for two weeks. I'm kinda like a fish out of water here. It's sure different from the big city. As much as early disclosers scare the britches off me, I think I can open up to you. You've got a real kind face. I came here to escape my ex. He sure was handy with his fists. "

I looked at this handsome man who was almost touching my thigh. Although he smiled, there was pain in his eyes. And for some reason, he'd shared his truth with me. Maybe he *was* right, and I was just a friendly face. But for the first time since meeting Wayne, I felt guilty about the thoughts that were going through my head. A big part of me wanted to swivel over, stroke his face with the back of my hand, and kiss him. But this was wrong. While trying to push these thoughts out of my head, I said,

"I'm sorry to hear about your ex. He sounds like a nasty piece of shit. I'm sure that you are already aware, but there's counselling support out there. There's no shame in asking for help. I can give you some numbers if you like. It's really easy to make friends here too. My partner and I worked in London for a while. People down there are very reserved until you get to know them. Wayne and I worked at a large hospital near the Thames. "

He blinked and recoiled into the chair. It didn't look like there were going to be any Anglo-American relationships developing any time soon. He swigged his coffee and looked at his watch. "Jesus, is that the time? I'd better get to surgery. It was a real pleasure meeting you. Wayne sure is one lucky man. You're one of the good ones. It'd be an honour to help you with your study. We'll arrange for you to shadow me in surgery and on my home visits. You've kinda got to get your hours signed off, haven't you?"

Sam was right. I needed to get my supervised practice hours signed off. It was part of my training. But that's *all* I required from him. Right now, I just wanted to get home to Wayne. When I got in, I nearly fell head first over Pongo to hug him. As his arms wrapped around me, I breathed deeply and contemplated telling Wayne about my encounter with the doctor. But nothing had really happened and the situation was under control. And anyway, not every-one needs to know about everything.

# Chapter Nineteen

I had no idea just how cruel this Victorian lady could be. She must've taken lessons from her cousin, the City infirmary. Life was going on as usual. A part of me liked the Belle Reve, even if it meant batting off Sam's brand of clinical support from time to time. By hook or crook, I was flying through my course and had somehow made it into my last year of training. Although we'd never become friends, I even learnt to tolerate Debbie. Pam, my predecessor, had officially left her role. Following her secondment opportunity, a substantive post had become available. And this meant an advanced nurse practitioner hole opened up permanently at the Belle Reve. But I was a trainee and for the time being, that was more than enough.

It annoyed me when I watched Debbie and Sarah in action. They giggled like two naughty school girls at the most inappropriate times. You didn't need to be Miss Marple to see that even the staff were sick of them. The nurses walked past these two hyenas, shaking their heads or raising their eyebrows. I often thought of my time at the Eastfield when Carla was my deputy. Out on the ward, I was friendly with everyone. We saved our personal relationship for behind closed doors and out of work. Sarah was not a patch on Carla. Although she may have not looked out of place on a runway, she was as fake as a three-pence coin. She didn't fool me with her pinned blonde hair, perfect make-up and slim hips either. If anything, she brought a whole new meaning to passive-aggression. This mouthpiece stuck her head out of the office and said,

"Max, I need you to prescribe Cyril some morphine injections to settle him. He's in so much pain. I've already phoned and spoken to Sam and he agrees with my decision. So off you pop and do it."

"Sarah, what do you mean?" I said whilst trying to ignore her curling lip. "He was stable when I left last night?"

"Are you questioning me, sunshine? I've told you that the patient is unwell and that should be enough. I've asked you nicely to do it. Perhaps I'll call the doctors at the surgery then and tell them you have refused."

"Sarah, you can call the prime minister for all I care. Don't you dare try to pull rank with me, sweetheart. Remember, I've done your job! We'll make decisions based on sound clinical assessment and not because of your demands. I'll review Cyril and get back to you. And feel free to go running to Debbie if you like. I couldn't give a monkeys chuff." And with that, I turned on my heel and left her with her mouth hanging open.

Cyril had chronic obstructive pulmonary disease. While he was taking oral antibiotics and steroids to help with an infection, his blood results and clinical presentation showed that he was responding to this treatment. When I left the night before, he was sitting up in bed, and talking. He only needed his oxygen occasionally now. His nebulised medication was also doing the trick to keep his lungs open. He didn't complain of any pain that wasn't controlled well with his usual 'as required' tablets. I couldn't understand what was going on. On entering his room, he was lying flat on his back and could hardly move. Someone had removed his nurse call from his reach. I immediately jumped into action. Once sat bolt upright, and after a nebuliser and a whiff of oxygen, he was back to his usual self. Although there were a few more secretions than normal because of his posture, his chest sounds were usual for him. There was no evidence of a clot in his lungs. An electrocardiogram showed nothing we didn't already know and, if anything, his oxygen levels were improving.

Cyril looked at me and said, "Oh, that feels better, Max. Thank you. I only buzzed to use the bottle."

"What do you mean?"

"I just wanted a Jimmy riddle."

It took me a while to get his history as the poor man was frightened. Apparently, a nurse had lowered his headrest, tutted and left the room. She had left him lying flat in sodden sheets. Alarm bells rang. Why would some-one put a breathless patient in this position? According to Cyril, the nurse had blond hair and was dressed in a navy blue uniform. Words failed me. For the first time in a very long time, I tasted vomit in my mouth. It took me around five minutes to find my feet. Once I'd settled him, I left his side room and tried to walk down the central corridor without giving the game away.

As I passed Sarah's office she said, "Well, have you done it? That poor man needs morphine and no one should have to suffer." I'll never know how I kept my cool. I looked at this monster and wanted to shake her. You're a nurse. How could you do that, you sick bitch? How can you stand there in that uniform and try to smile at me? My heart raced as fast as my thoughts. She continued, "I'm sorry about earlier. You're right, I shouldn't have shouted at you or tried to threaten you with the doctor. That was so unprofessional. It's just that I care about these patients and want them to be comfortable. I'll draw up the morphine now, shall I?"

"No, I've not prescribed it. Let me just run to the toilet and I'll be back in a few minutes. I've been crossing my legs all morning. You know how busy we all are. You don't want a puddle in your office, do you now?" That was the best excuse I could find, but somehow she bought it. I'd never put on a better show in my entire life as I smiled and left.

I couldn't remember how I'd climbed the staircase and reached my office. The phone felt hot in my hands as I gripped onto the receiver for sheer life. Jan cancelled her meetings and rushed over to me. I thought it was strange that Sarah's ward had been experiencing a surge of ill patients. The unexpected symptoms all had one thing in common: they appeared suddenly and without warning. There were instances of severely low blood sugars in diabetic patients who usually have good control over their insulin. Additionally, there were drowsy patients with no logical explanation and a few cases of cardiac arrests occurring outside of regular hours. And now there was this. Although the incidents were reported and independently investigated, no one had connected the dots between these unexplained events. Until this point, I had never imagined that there could even be the possibility of a link between these mysterious illnesses. It just didn't bare thinking about. It was horrific. Every second felt like a minute and every minute felt like an hour. I sat by my computer and blankly stared at the screen. In less than ten minutes, Jan was sitting across from me. In just fifteen minutes, Sarah was removed from the ward and suspended. Within twenty minutes, Carla had been called from the Eastfield to step in and within thirty minutes, I had seen my breakfast for the second time that day.

It was no surprise that Debbie had denied any prior knowledge of the issues. But how could she see what was happening when she was so oblivious? She spent all her time gossiping with her friend instead of paying attention to the patients and staff. Conveniently, a position suddenly opened up in training at the City Infirmary. There would be less room for her to go unnoticed there. From bitter experience, I knew the hospital gossip would have a field day with Debbie's downfall, but I didn't care. My focus was on the patients and staff at Bell Reve. The police took over the investigation, but despite providing counselling and supervision for the staff, the situation remained horrific. The idea of a nurse harming people was unfathomable. Despite her faults, I knew deep down that there was only one person who could help me through this. I picked up the telephone, waited for the line to connect, and then said,

"Danni, it's Max, can you chat?"

"Of course, anytime."

"It's not something that I can say over the phone," I explained. "Are you free this evening to pop over for a bit?"

"Yes, I'll tell Malc that I've had a better offer. We'll have to go line dancing another time. It's no big deal. I'll be there about eight."

I was desperate to see her. If anyone could help me, then it was Danni, the champion of the world. She crept in past Pongo and found Wayne and me sitting at the kitchen table. Her hand casually rested on my shoulder as she sat down. While Wayne poured the brew, I said,

"Danni, thanks so much for coming over. I just didn't know who to call. Wayne is amazing, he really is, but I wanted to speak to another nurse. Carla has enough on her plate at the moment trying to support a devastated team and also help Poppy run the ward at the Eastfield. And that's without Jack Junior thrown into the mix for good measure.

"I just can't sleep. Every time I close my eyes, I think of Sarah and what she's done. I'm doing my best to keep it together at work, but I'm a mess. Why would someone want to hurt patients? It will traumatise their poor families as well. I keep on thinking about how long it has been going on for and how many people she could've hurt over the years.

"It left me cold when Sarah tried to justify her actions when the police interviewed her. The sicko thought she was doing every-one a favour by freeing up bed capacity. Her words haunt me. She really believed that the patients had lived too long. And there she was, trying to bully staff into prescribing medication that wasn't needed by inducing symptoms. How did she get away with that? I just don't know. What a completely sick, murdering bitch."

Danni grabbed hold of my hand. "Max, you did the right thing. Always remember that. I dread to think about what would have happened. I don't know why she did it either. But I'm glad you stopped her in her tracks. I know we are like cat and dog sometimes, but always remember that I have your back."

Tears trundled down my cheeks. It was odd. It took me by surprise. I hadn't cried like this since Jack had died. And then it was more than tears. I was sobbing. Sometimes, words are unnecessary. Danni gripped my hand a little tighter. But I wasn't the only one in the room crying.

The staff took to Carla like a duck to water. She was just herself; kind and approachable. Within six months, she'd completely turned the ward around. Her team was happy knowing that their 'hands-on' ward manager was just one of them. Nothing was too much trouble, and no problem was too small for her to sort out. It was as if she had infused the very fibre of Belle Reve with her brand of down-to-earth friendliness. Equally, Poppy was going from strength to strength at the Eastfield.

"What is it duck?" I asked on the way out of the hospital. "Has Jack Junior been playing you up? You look absolutely beat."

"You're right, he's a bloody handful, but that's just kids for you. I need eyes in my backside, he's into everything. But no, it's not him, Max."

Somehow, I found my arm around her shoulder. Even after an eight-hour shift, I still detected a faint whiff of her usual perfume as I brought her closer to me. "Well, what is it then? Don't tell me you are pregnant again. Is that it?"

"Good God, no," she laughed, "we want more kids, but not just yet. Christian is up for promotion and I'm - "

"- you're what? What is it, Carla?"

"Don't get your knickers in a twist, Max. It's nothing bad. Jan came to see me the other day. I've been meaning to talk to you about it. But I've been running around like a headless chicken on the ward and never got the chance to chat with you. We've both been busy. She told me that the matron post is going up for advert soon."

"That's brilliant news, Carla. You must go for it," I said whilst hugging her a little tighter. "Anyway, while we are putting our cards on the table, I've some news too."

Now seemed as good as any time to tell her. "I'm nearly done with my training here. All in all, it's been great fun, and I've learnt so much. But the thing is, I don't want to stay. I've had a chat with Jan and put her in the picture. Luckily, she understands. You know me, Carla, I never do things the easy way.

"I want to be an untouchable. My office is slap bang next to the community matron team. On the quiet, I've shadowed a few of them. This has helped to get my practice hours signed off. They're quite normal when you get to know them. It's a brilliant job. I love the thought of bringing health care to people's homes who can't access it in the traditional way.

"And it just happens that one of the team is leaving. Her husband has got a job in Cumbria so they are selling up. This leaves a vacancy and I really want to give it a go. The competition will be tough but If I don't try, I'll never know. Whilst it'd be comfortable to stay at the Belle Reve, I'm too young for a pipe and a pair of slippers.

"Anyway, the penny's just bloody dropped. If you do get the matron post, then you'll be my boss. And I'm certainly not having any of that. You know where you can stick your 'nursing tool bag speech'."

"I certainly do." I could almost taste what was left of her cherry lip gloss on my cheek as we both collapsed into fits of giggles. "The second shelf to the left. But joking apart, I'm pleased that you are following your heart. Just do what makes you happy. I get it. If someone gave you a million pounds, you would want a million and one. "

Carla was right, even if as subtle as a brick. But it wasn't necessarily a bad thing that I always tried to prove myself. Without this need for validation, I fear which gutter I would've ended up lying in.

# Chapter Twenty

Society was changing. Margaret Thatcher's section 28 was out, and Tony Blair's civil partnership act was in. The Civil Partnership Act formally recognised our relationship within statutory organisations. This groundbreaking legislation granted civil partners the same rights as married couples in terms of property, tenancy, social security, pension benefits, exemptions, inheritance tax, life insurance, and next-of-kin rights in hospitals. Finally, our love had security, rights, and legal recognition. And to be honest, it all felt surreal. Because as much as I tried, in my darker moments, I still tasted sea salt on my lips and heard Blanche playing songs in my head. I'd lived in the shadows of that Cornish Cliffe face far too long to know any difference.

Even watching the good, the bad and the damn right ugly reactions to the legislation discussed on the news didn't cement it in my head. Mrs Thatcher's bloodstained knife still gave me phantom pain, with or without the amputation. Wayne grabbed hold of my hand. "What's the matter, babe? Why are you crying?"

The television images flickered into our living room, casting shadows across the wall. But this didn't mean it was real, did it? Pongo pushed between us as I wiped my face with a tissue. "Don't get me wrong Wayne. I'm as happy as a dog with two dicks about the whole thing. It just triggers all sorts of shit in my head. I thought I'd moved on. Why did we have to go through all of that in the first place? That Thatcher bitch has a lot to answer for."

"There's no point in holding onto it, Max. It'll only make you spiral again."

What had he just said to me? Had I just heard him right? There was no need to rub the past in my face. I pulled away from him and felt my nostrils flaring. I said, "What exactly do you mean by that?"

"I mean the past doesn't have to define your future. It's quite sad to watch."

"Sad, eh? Thank you very fucking much!"

I hadn't seen his eyes narrow and change to this shade of black for a very long time. And then he went in for the kill. "That's not what I meant, and well you know it. Stop twisting my fucking words. I was trying to pay you a compliment, but like always, you've taken it the wrong way. Don't do this to me. I'm not the fucking enemy here. You're good enough. It's a crying shame that your parents didn't feel the same way. And that was long before Daniel had his grubby hands in your mental health.

"I'm no-one to talk. That'd be the cat calling the kettle black. You know better than any-one else that I'm work in progress. Just look at what happened in London. I don't want to argue with you. I love you."

Pongo whimpered, and my red mist had gone. What the fuck had I done? Wayne was shaking. I was no different from bloody Danni. "I love you too, and I'm sorry. I've screwed this up, haven't I?"

"Well, yes and no. It's cleared the air," he said whilst comforting Pongo.

Deep down, I wanted to enter into a civil partnership with Wayne. That was a given. But part of me was ashamed. How could I prance down the aisle in view of our friends and family if I didn't believe that I deserved it? When my mother found out that I was gay, her last parting words before throwing me out onto the streets were,

*"If I knew what you were when you were growing inside me, then I would have got rid of you and had you aborted."*

No amount of therapy, trauma trawling, shouting, drinking or trying to find my purpose through work appeased these demons. And now and again, they surged to the surface.

---

There is nothing like a change in scenery and a bit of exercise to put things into perspective. Gold and ruby shades blew around us as we played 'piggy in the middle' with Pongo on the soggy field. It took him approximately three seconds flat to have us both covered from head to foot in muddy ball splatter. I was just grateful that I was wearing my old dog-walking clothes. Pongo hurtled towards me and forgot to stop. Being on your back on a chilly autumn afternoon covered in dog slobber, laughter and love was the perfect therapy. The mud felt good under my back. That stinky dog seemed to understand exactly what I needed, even before I did.

Wayne and I sat in the bathtub together. Lavender bubbles infused with droplets of bourbon dripped down the cream tiles in the candlelight. But as romantic as it was, somehow I'd got the tap end again. Pongo sat upright with his head resting on the side of the bath between us. Wayne tapped my leg and said,

"There's no pressure from me either way. However, we could scroll through the internet later if you fancy it. Let's just see what's out there. If we decide to go ahead, it should be very low key and simple."

I drew love hearts with soap on his thigh. "Yes, ok, let's find out a bit more. I don't want to be on show. That's not me at all."

Once we'd finished wrinkling in the tub, we searched the internet for the right venue within our budget. The whole thing just had to be easy. The perfect location had been under our noses for years without us even knowing. There was many a time that we had walked Pongo past the Regent Hotel. This white building sat within spitting distance of the Queen's Park on the outskirts of town. The hotel would be big enough to house our guests, but small enough to be intimate. But best of all, it wasn't trying to be anything that it wasn't. It seemed odd seeing a link to both weddings and civil partnership packages on their website.

"Well, what do you think, Max? I'll go at your pace. Do you want to mull it over?"

"No, babe, I need to get over myself."

"We can just go to the registrar's office with a couple of witnesses, if you prefer?"

"No, that just seems so cold. We need to strike a balance."

Carrie, a woman in her thirties with a black bob, waited for us in the panelled hotel reception. Crimson lipstick punctuated her angular features. She wore a smart grey pinstriped trouser suit and a pink blouse. To the right of the reception desk was a door leading to the bar. If you turned left, you would enter a beautifully appointed restaurant with views of Queens Park. Each time the door swung open, my stomach growled. A red carpet connected the rooms, creating a seamless flow. I had read on their website that the hotel used to be a coaching inn in its heyday. The Regent was renowned back then. Since then, the rear stables and courtyard were now a carpark and additional guest rooms. I felt so comfortable in the hotel's faded grandeur.

"Good afternoon, gentleman, you must be Max and Wayne. It's a pleasure to meet you and welcome to the Regent," Carrie said.

"Yes, we are, it's great to meet you too", I replied. And then we followed her into the bar.

A smartly dressed barman in a maroon waistcoat, white shirt and black trousers brought over the complimentary drinks to our booth. I admired his attention to detail. He wiped the table and carefully placed a clean beer mat before setting down the glasses of coke. His green eyes glinted at Carrie. She cleared her throat and said,

"Well, it's really nice to have you here. It's about time that the law changed. We've done a few civil partnerships over the last few months." She gestured towards the barman who was now polishing glasses and shouted, "It's quite a family affair here. Only last month, we hosted my brother's civil partnership. We did that handsome brute over there proud, didn't we, Tom?"

He laughed, flicked his black fringe out of his eyes and said, "You certainly did, sis. Carl and I were over the moon."

Now turning her attention to us, she said, "What do you have in mind? We can do anything to make it a special day. I'll give you a proper tour of the hotel and the function rooms shortly."

Wayne and I looked at each other. I felt him grab my hand under the table. We'd actually made a list of what we didn't want, instead of focusing on what we did. However, this was a good starting point. I said,

"This is all very new to us, so we're in your hands. Wayne and I have been chatting. We like the package that includes the evening buffet and disco."

"Oh yes, that's very popular. Not every-one wants a formal sit-down meal. We'll have the ceremony in the function room. Then we'll re-arrange the space whilst you and your guests are having photos taken. When you return from the Queen's Park, everything will be ready for cake cutting, speeches, and the first dance. A hot buffet and disco will follow.

"This package includes enough fizz for each guest to have a couple of glasses. You'll stay for the night in one of our premium rooms with views of Queens Park. We'll even throw in breakfast before you check out the next morning.

"I'll be here for the whole thing and make sure it goes like clockwork. That's my job. You won't have to worry about a thing. Once I know your colours, wishes, flowers, order of service, music for the ceremony and any specific wishes, then you can leave everything to me.

"I'll be at your side, but not in the way. We'll make sure that we have the registrar booked in advance. The council has just employed a new senior one. If you're lucky, then she may conduct the service herself. She's lovely. I think her name is Jayne. When you make an appointment at the office, ask for her. She was amazing with my handsome brother."

Suddenly, any anxieties had vanished. Carrie was exactly what we were looking for. "Thanks. We only want a small do with around thirty to forty people. Can we keep it quite simple?"

"That's fine Max, we'll do whatever we need to do to make the day personal for you and Wayne. Now let's have a look at the function rooms. I've kept you chatting here because we've just set the room up for an evening reception. Let's just sneak in whilst the wedding party is having their pictures taken. You'll see everything that we do here for yourselves. Jane, our other events planner, has organised this one, but we work in exactly the same way. At the moment, she's in full swing, making sure that the wedding goes well."

We were led into one of the function rooms at the back of the hotel. It looked beautiful in a Disney princess sort of way. Carousel tables surrounded a small dance floor. Silver tablecloths shimmered against the central candelabras of lilac candles and plumes of large-headed hydrangeas. The staff had draped each chair with a silver cover, complete with a large lilac bow. The team had scattered foliage and fake lilac rose petals over the tables. A door swished open behind us. Large silver carvers full of buffet food wafted in. Waiters delicately placed them at the end of a long table in a separate annexe just off to the left of the dance floor. My mouth watered as the kitchen staff placed large dishes of hot food in a Bay Marie.

Carrie asked, "Well, what do you think?"

Wayne grabbed hold of my hand. "Max, is this what you have in mind? It's all fine by me, but I just want you to be happy."

"Yes, the food looks perfect and smells so good. I don't want to be horrible as it's a personal choice, but I think the table decorations need to be stripped back a bit for us. We can have a bit of something, but I don't want all of this glitz. I'm not criticising though."

"Yes, I agree. Sometimes, less is more," he said.

Carrie smiled. "We'll do whatever you want. My brother didn't go big on the table decorations either. Now, would you like to sample some of the buffet food? I've asked our chef to put a selection on a hot plate. Go to the dining room and I'll bring it through. I'll give you a proforma too. Just fill it in over the next few weeks, return it to me, and I'll organise a contract if you want to go ahead."

By the time we had finished the food, we'd made our decision. The Regent would host our civil partnership and that was that.

*I have never felt like this, for once I'm lost for words, your smile has really thrown me.* We stood outside the ceremony room door and watched our guests through the crack. We laughed as Carla was doing her best to stop Jack Junior from picking the red roses from the registrar's table. *This is not like me at all, I'd never thought I'd know the kind of love you've shown me.* Wayne looked incredibly handsome. Instead of purchasing wedding gear that we knew we wouldn't wear again, we decided to rent matching black morning suits. *Now, no matter where I am, no matter what I do, I see your face appearing.* Danni had bought us pins that shimmered against our burgundy silk cravats. Gone were Wayne's long locks and in was a short brown quiff. Although it was difficult for me to see it go, he was right; it was time for a change. *Like an unexpected song, an unexpected song, that only we are hearing.* I gripped hold of his hands and kissed him. You could cut the atmosphere with a knife as the music changed. It was showtime. *Some say love, it is a river that drowns the tender reed.* Carrie pushed open the doors and Jayne announced,

"Please be upstanding every-one for Wayne and Max."

*Some say love, it is a razor that leaves your soul to bleed. Some say love, it is a hunger, an endless aching need.* I clenched Wayne's hand and my legs turned to jelly. As we walked into the room, our guests gasped. Through our tears, all we felt was love and acceptance. *I say love it is a flower and you it's only seed.* I can't remember how we got from the back of the room to the front. *It's the heart afraid of breaking that never learns to dance.* Everyone was there who we loved and cared about. And that was more than enough for both of us. Wayne gently nudged me as we arrived at the front of the room. He was looking over at Carla, Christian, and Jack Junior. Then I understood what he was trying to tell me. Saint Peter had given Jack and Michael a free pass for the day. They must've done something unspeakable to be allowed through the pearly gates once more. Only God knows what it was. They huddled together next to Jack Junior. From the corner of my eye, I watched them wave. It was odd. Jack Junior chuckled at his uncle and waved too.

Aunt Bren was magnificent. She had the grace and poise of a slim Dame Edna Everage as she stood at the front of the room, chatting with our guests. It was just a pity that we'd opted for roses rather than gladioli. As she moved, her fake purple fur coat slipped from her shoulders. Maybe it wanted to cock its leg up a lamppost? Eventually, she took it off, revealing a lilac-fitted silk dress. The dress had a plunging neckline and sequins adorning the hem. She looked like an aging geisha girl who had fallen into a drag queen's jewellery box. Only Aunt Bren could carry off such fabulousness. Through her heavily mascaraed eyes and thick red lipstick, she said,

"It's bloody amazing to celebrate the love of Max and Wayne here today. They're a blinking beautiful couple that deserve to be happy together. I'd be lost without the pair of silly buggers. Before I completely ruin my face, I'd like to read a few lyrics from an Erasure song that means a lot to them.

> *Open your eyes, I see*
> *Your eyes are open.*
> *Wear no disguise for me*
> *Come into the open,*

*When it's cold outside*
*Am I here in vain?*
*Hold on to the night*
*There will be no shame,*
*Always, I wanna be with you*
*And make believe with you*
*And live in harmony, harmony, oh love.*

Now, please excuse me all. I need to sit down and touch up my mascara again. Trust me, you don't want to see me without my make-up. Think of the Bride of Dracula meets a piece of old leather." There was a low giggle in the room as she sat down next to me. I looked at her and simply kissed her cheek before Jayne called us for the 'I - do' part.

And just before the formal proceedings happened, I heard a familiar song blurt out over the speakers. *I saw my love walking down the aisle and as he passed me by; he turned and smiled.* I whispered in Wayne's ear, "No, you haven't. You said that she couldn't come, you sod."

Wayne looked at me and laughed. "As I say, Max, not everyone needs to know everything. Nancy wouldn't miss this for the world. Don't blame just me. We've all been in on it." *And as he passed me by, he turned and smiled.* All eyes darted to the back of the room as the one and only Miss Nancy Eclair catapulted through the door in three-inch silver heals, a white shimmering wedding dress and an even bigger blonde wig than I had ever seen her wear before. Her long lace veil flowed behind her like Batman's cape. *The preacher joined their hands and all the people began to stand.* And she still carried that netted bag of foam bricks. She traipsed down the centre aisle, picking up the red rose petals and shoving them down her breast plate in disgust. When the mood took her, she stopped, and either sat and gyrated on a man's lap or hit someone with her bag. *You know it should have been me, instead of her walking to you.* As I waited for this pregnant six-foot bride to take her angst out on me again, I cried. Every now and again, I caught her eye. Although she faked anger, all I could really see was love. She hadn't lost her touch and certainly was still a lip-sync assassin. Within about two seconds flat, her audience was eating out of her hand as she knocked seven shades out of me with her foam bricks. *Now you're standing there saying 'I-do', holding hands with somebody new.* She collapsed to the floor and hung around my ankles. At one point, I thought I was going to lose my trousers. Our guests were in stitches. *Darling, how could you do this to me?* But it certainly wasn't my fault that I had jilted her for the third time in a row. Some girls just never learn. This routine hadn't changed, but society certainly had since the early days at the European Bar. As she rose to her feet, she batted her beautiful long beaded lashes and said,

"Surprise! You didn't think that Miss Nancy would miss this, did you? You're my family. Now please excuse me while I slip into something comfier. That boring little man, Adam, will be along shortly to spend the evening with you all. I'm so sorry, he's the personality of a draft excluder, so just bare with him if you will, my darling boys. I'd better go before I steal the show. Mwah, mwah."

She was right. It was difficult to top that. The rest of the service was simple compared to her intrusion. After the 'I-do's, we embraced and our guests cheered. It felt like heaven. But being upstaged by Nancy was beautifully poignant. As we walked back up the aisle, Jack blew a kiss and formed a heart shape with his sausage fingers. Then he slowly faded away with Michael. They must've been called back by Saint Peter for some organ work. After the photographer was done, Carrie called Wayne and me into the reception room. It was perfect. Simple, white, crisp tablecloths covered the tables. Red roses tied with black organza ribbon were enough. A few red hearts and rose petals scattered the tabletops. It was a good thing I wasn't wearing mascara. A groom with panda eyes is never a good look.

Everyone was having a great time. Dylan, George, Maria, and Laura were dancing to Britney Spears and Destiny's Child. Len watched from the safety of the bar as they threw their moves. Danni and Malc quickly joined the dance floor when "Cotton Eye Joe" started playing. The multi-coloured disco lights pulsed with the music. Danni was really going all out, with the strobes reflecting off her silver sequenced dress and dancing parrots. We clapped along as they recreated Nashville. Adam later took Aunt Bren to the floor, lip-syncing to 'I Will Survive.' He looked like Prince Charming in a blue linen suit, and she was his Cinderella. I couldn't tell who had more makeup on though. Carla and Christian joined the crowd, while Jack Junior kept bouncing between Wayne and me. He was obsessed with our cravats, trying to get the rhinestone pins from the centre.

My white dress shirt was totally stuck to me by the end of the evening. And whilst this wasn't a great look, I couldn't of cared less. More to the point, neither did Wayne. Every time we sat down, someone dragged us back up or plied us with booze. I was itching to get in that corner jacuzzi with him and see what came up. But all of that would wait until our friends had their fill of drink, food and disco. This was definitely one of those orange bag moments. Well, it would if I'd had the coordination to actually hold a netted bag. Not even Arnold could manage that in this state. The room swayed, our family danced, and for the first time in ages, I felt content.

# Chapter Twenty-One

A hue of purple pleasure punctuated Bren's boudoir. Instead of a lava lamp, there was now one of those new-fangled aromatherapy diffusers sitting on her dressing table. This LED-lit lilac extravaganza had all the bells and whistles. You'd never guess that from its delicate tulip-shaped stem, it could spew out mist into the room like an old steam engine. This gadget was so potent, it even outdid her Avon perfume bottles. She smirked and turned her new toy up to full pelt. When Max gave her this vibrating plastic contraption, she was dumbfounded. Equally, Bren knew when to keep her mouth shut. And at least she wasn't getting her fingers burnt on that old lamp now. Soothing lavender and Lionel Ritchie floated over her bedroom. Oh, the things she could do to that man if given half the chance. Well, that is, once her anti-inflammatories had kicked in. He sounded even smoother on the new compact disc player that the girls at work had given her. It was such a thoughtful retirement gift from the majestic domestic team. *I've been alone with you inside my mind. And in my dreams, I've kissed your lips a thousand times.* If she had anything to do with it, she would kiss far more than just his lips. The very thought of Lionel set her off again. *Hello, is it me you're looking for?* Well, a girl needs to have dreams.

It was the end of an era. Bren had hung up her orange uniform and high duster for good. There was a throng of excited cackles echoing along the ground-floor corridors of the nursing home. Staff lined the panelled walls to form an arch of cardboard urinals. She never even smelt a rat until it was too late. And by then, a bandage-clad chariot of fire was waiting for her. Mrs 'M' told her to plonk her bum in the wheelchair whilst a scrum of porters serenaded her to Rod Stewart's 'Da Ya Think I'm Sexy?' The bloody cheek of them. It was a given that she was and always would be. And more to the point, they of all people should have known just how sexy she was, especially as she'd buffed up more than just the tables in the Porters Lodge for years.

A festoon of blue streamers did their best to glisten under an old mirror ball. Just like Bren, it'd seen better days, but still tried to cast its spell over the party. Wait a minute, the streamers were exactly the same shade as the hospital blue roll. For more years than she cared to remember, she'd wiped this Victorian lady's rear with this paper. The staff had ordered a hot buffet, and it proudly sat steaming on large plates that were usually reserved for passing dignitaries. Anyone who was anyone was waiting for Bren to make her grand entrance. You see, the infirmary looked after its own. Sharron Varley and Emily Dickson pushed the stained glass doors aside for Bren to enter. There were peels of 'Surprise' followed by 'for she's a jolly good scrubber' ringing out from most of the hospital staff. But Emily Dickson was having none of it. Such vulgarity had no place in a hospital.

Bren nearly fell out of her wheelchair in delight. If only someone had tipped her off. She would've definitely worn her new waterproof mascara and her latest Avon perfume. But the heady aroma of hospec and her everyday scent still overpowered her guests. Just before shoving a hot sausage roll into her mouth, she spotted me lurking behind the door, talking to Carla. Her arm jangled towards me. "Max, I'll bloody kill you. Did you know about this too?"

"Now don't blame me. I wasn't the only culprit. Just look around. I think Danni is here somewhere too."

She laughed, swallowed half of the sausage roll, and then placed a greasy kiss on my cheek. It was a real art form watching her trying to speak without spitting puff pastry everywhere. Eventually, she slobbered, "You bloody fool! I love the lot of you."

"And we love you too. Now show 'em how to do it properly."

She grabbed hold of one of the young blonde porters and lead him to the dance floor. In about three seconds flat, our retirement girl was hanging off his neck as her Lionel belted out 'All Night Long.' If only. She was old enough to be this poor lad's grandmother. But if nothing else, God loves a trier. As people slowly faded away from the party, I scooped her up, placed her in my VW, and safely delivered her to her first-floor flat. But as much as I knew she'd overdone it, there was no way that she was accepting my help. My heart was in my mouth as I watched her climb that steep staircase.

Bren sat in front of her dressing-table mirror and contemplated her future, now that she no longer had to work. She needed to come up with a 'Plan B' to carry her through retirement, just in case she didn't become Mrs Bren Ritchie, after all. But age was just a number. To her reckoning, she'd been counting backwards for at least the last fifteen years. Her purple nylon dressing gown felt good against her puckered skin. It was just the right side of respectable to cover her cleavage without looking trashy at the same time. There'd been many a time when she had flung it on and pranced down her stairs like a prima ballerina to answer the door without so much as an Ibuprofen in sight. But her flouncing days were well and truly over. That bloody diffuser was certainly doing its thing, even if it did steam up her mirror. Now that it was on full throttle, she felt like an older blonde version of Fenella Fielding in 'Carry On Screaming'. Bren never tired of watching that famous scene when Fenella famously asked Harry H. Corbett, "Do you mind if I smoke?"

Whilst she'd certainly entertained a few 'Odd Bods' on her satin sheets over the years, she was still technically alone. Well, you couldn't count her Alan, who still sat in his urn in the back of the rickety white wardrobe. And as much as she tried, she just wasn't ready to move him anywhere else. But there was something about his urn that she hated. This biscuit tin of a contraction still triggered memories of being stopped at customs when she returned with him from Spain. Maybe one day she'd find something that was more befitting to honour the memory of the only man that she'd truly loved. But there was no rush. He wasn't going anywhere soon. And anyway, it wasn't as if she could pop to the shops for a loaf of bread and call into the urn shop on her way back. It'd mean a purpose trip to the funeral directors. And there was only one way she planned to go over that threshold. But it certainly wasn't on her feet.

Goodness, where had the time gone? Max and Wayne would arrive soon. The last thing they needed was to see her in this state. Her bloody Mascara Gods had been ignoring her prayers again. One of these fine days, she'd get herself some of this Botox stuff. But until that day of reckoning finally arrived, it was war paint all the way. She sighed, leaned into the mirror, and took a better look at the devastation. To Lionel's dulcet tones, she rummaged through her best camouflage and tried to work a miracle once again. It was going to be a tough conversation. At least she could look her best when she dropped the bombshell. That bitch of a sister staring back at her in that grainy childhood picture certainly had a lot to answer for.

As we pulled up in the taxi, Aunt Bren was waiting on her doorstep. Her fake purple fur covered a lilac leopard print figure-hugging dress. And for her age, she certainly still had it. She smiled through crimson lipstick and purple eyeshadow. God knows why she'd made all of this effort. We were only off for a meal and a couple of drinks at the Potter's Arms. But as long as she was happy, then that was enough for me. Whilst trying to kiss her without getting caught in her rather large drop leaf earrings and matching choker, I said,

"Well, don't you look the glamourous aunt. It's so good to see you. Are you fit?"

"Actually boys, if it's not too much trouble, can we have a quiet night in at your place? I'm sure that this young strapping man here will drive us to the takeaway curry house on the way."

"That's no problem, Aunt Bren. Are you feeling poorly?"

"No, not at all Max. I thought it would be nice to have a curry and chat for a change. Sometimes, I find it difficult to make out what's being said over the noise of the pub. I bet Wayne has the same problem, don't you duck?"

Wayne turned to face us and said, "You're spot on there, Bren. I spend most of my time trying to lip-read you all. It's hard work, though."

She smiled and tapped the driver on the shoulder. "Well, that's settled then. Take us to the curry house and step on it. I have a chicken tikka masala with my name on it."

Everyone in the car laughed as we sped off. Pongo was pleased to see us when we got back. Instead of jumping all over us, he slowly rose from his bed and slumped over to say hello. He was still as beautiful as ever. If anything, his greying snout and eyelids made him look distinguished.

"Goodness me, this bloody naan bread is gorgeous," Aunt Bren said whilst ripping another piece off. "Come on boys, have some please before I scoff it all. When it comes to curry, I don't know when to stop."

I looked at her dipping the crusty bread into her feast. "I know. It's lovely, but not as gorgeous as you are. We don't know what we'd do without you."

"It's just as bloody well that I'm not planning on going anywhere soon, isn't it then?"

Once we'd finished our feast and washed the plates, we settled down in the living room with a brew. With a bit of help, Pongo got on the sofa and snuggled into his usual spot between Wayne and me. It wasn't long before I felt his familiar snore vibrate against my thigh.

Aunt Bren just couldn't get comfortable in her usual wing-backed chair. She squirmed on the cracked leather like she was next in line to have a tooth pulled without an anaesthetic. I looked over at her and said,

"Are you OK? Are you in pain or something? Do you need me to get you anything?"

She shook her head. "I'm sorry boys, as much as I've enjoyed the curry and your company, I've got you here under false pretences. I've been dreading this."

"Dreading what? I'm worried. What's wrong?"

She sipped her drink and slapped it down on a coaster. "I don't know where to start with it all. Just let me ramble 'till I make sense.

The other day, I received a phone call from your sister. Apparently, she's had my number for years. I think she lifted it from one of your mother's old phone address books before she left. I nearly died of shock when I heard her voice. Can you remember her?"

"Of course I can. We were close. When my mother threw me out, she told me not to come anywhere near Anna again or else-"

"- or else what Max, did she threaten you?"

"Yes, she told me she knew some very nasty people," I explained.

"That piggin' woman never fails to surprise me. I know she's your mother, but she's nothing but a bitch. How low can you go to threaten your son like that? You never told me that before."

"But what does any of this have to do with Anna phoning you out of the blue?"

She shook her head and went on, "Your mother told Anna that it was *you* who wanted nothing to do with her. You should've heard Anna her when I put her straight. She's missed you so much, but all this time believed you didn't want to see her.

"I know where Karen got that sick trick from. Our mother, Annie, did exactly the same thing with the two of us when we were growing up. She played us both like a bloody fiddle to get what she wanted. But that certainly doesn't give my sister an excuse for her cruelty. She could've been such a good mother if she'd put her mind to it. If someone has hurt you, then you have two choices. You can either choose to be a survivor like me, or you can be a victim like your mother.

"Karen is still the angry girl who is hurting inside. Let's just say that Grandma Annie and Grandad Sid could have taught Myra Hindley and Ian Brady a thing or two. But anyway, sorry, this isn't about me. I'm losing my thread again. Max, there's no easy way of saying this. Anna has breast cancer. She wants to see you."

What? Wasted years built on lies. A dog lick. Wayne's heavy arm on my shoulder. Shivering. Fuck, which way was up? My head hurts. My sister thinks I rejected her. She has cancer. My mother's a bitch. Aunt Bren told me why. Shit, curry curdling in my stomach. Quick upstairs. Shaking. Wrenching. Lumps of orange and yellow. Relief. Luckily, the buzz of the extractor fan hid my sobs. Just before I spiralled down the rabbit hole, there was a thump at the door. Wayne shouted over the fan, "Are you alright in there, Max? We're worried about you."

"Yes, I'm much better now, sorry," I said, opening the door with minty fresh breath. "It was just the shock of it all babe. Just go down to Aunt Bren. I'll be with you in a minute."

After a glass of cold water, I sat back down. "Aunt Bren, what else did Anna say to you? I want to know everything. It's OK, just tell me."

She took a deep breath and continued, "Anna escaped and has not been back to your parent's home since training as a policewoman. She now lives with her partner, Dawn, near Manchester. Before she met Dawn, I think she was shacked up with a man named Carl. He wasn't very nice to her. She didn't go into lots of detail on the phone, but I'm sure that she'll tell you about it when she's ready. The only good thing to come out of that relationship was your nephews. Anna has two little boys. I think she said the eldest is around nine and the youngest is about six. Max, you're an uncle.

She's desperate to see you and wants to introduce you both to her kids. I've told her a little about you, but have only skimmed the details. She knows about Wayne. You can fill in the rest when you see her."

All of this had gone on in some parallel world and I'd been oblivious. I'd closed the box marked 'Anna' in my head, as it had been too painful to open. I really thought that my mother had locked it tight and had thrown away the key. Aunt Bren looked as if she didn't know whether to laugh or cry. I smiled at her and said, "Thanks for telling me. I can see why you were nervous."

"Nervous? I've been bricking myself duck. I think that some-one upstairs is having a giraffe. No-one was more shocked than me when I heard Anna's voice. But, it sounds like that she has been through the ringer from what she said. And that's without the cancer. Oh, those poor kids."

But Aunt Bren was right. Those little boys must be beside themselves with worry. Stuff it. Why had I been trying to climb the greasy pole at work for so long and focussing all of my energy there? None of it mattered in the grand scheme of things. I'd done a complete three-sixty in a matter of seconds and had never been happier. I knew exactly what to do next.

# Chapter Twenty-Two

I've never liked the motorway. All of those speeding idiots, the smell of pollution on my breath and, of course, the traffic jams turned me off. My stomach did a double loop every time one of those juggernauts juddered past us. Just look at what had happened to Carla and Christian. And that wasn't even on three lanes of hell. But today, I just wanted to get there as quickly as possible. Luckily, Wayne agreed to drive. With a lot of bargaining with God, a liberal dose of 'rescue remedy' and prolific swearing, we arrived at my sister's home in just over an hour. Our 'bitch in the box', as I called her, had navigated us to a tree-lined street with views of a municipal crematorium and matching cemetery. It didn't click until we arrived why my sister lived on 'Grave-side Grove'. I looked over at my beautiful man and said,

"Is it safe to pull up here first please, babe? I don't want to get swept into the next funeral by mistake. It's literally one in, one out here. I want to find my land legs before we get to my sister's house. That bloody motorway has played havoc with my nerves. I'd rather do the 'Big-One' again at Blackpool Pleasure Beach before getting on that road to hell."

He scoffed, pulled into 'Pleasant Pines Crematoria' carpark and turned off the engine. "Max, you'll be fine. Anna can't wait to see you, remember? Don't stress. But, as you've brought it up, I've got my eye on another coaster. It's on my bucket list to ride the 'Hulk' at Universal's Islands of Adventure in Florida."

He knew that this was the distraction I needed. "And you with a hole in the heart. I know it's repaired but I don't fancy a repeat of 'Peter and the Dam'. You'll be a lot closer to your bucket if you go on that. I've heard it's extreme."

"Yes, I know that dummy," he said, shaking my leg, "but life is for living. Anyway, I'm not saying now, but I'd really like to go in the future."

We watched the next coffin slide into the crematorium conveyor belt. Wayne was right. Life can change in the bat of a beaded eyelash. "OK then, if that's what you really want to do. We'll have to save hard for it."

With thoughts of losing more than my inhibitions on a roller coaster, we crept out of the carpark. According to the sat nav, we'd be at our destination in around two minutes. I peered over the top of my sunglasses at a pebble-dashed bay-fronted prefab. A tidy privet and well-kept front lawn led to a white door. Telltale kids' bikes with muddy wheels were chained to the side of the house. I took a deep breath as I got out of the car, being careful not to step in anything on the side grass verge. It drives me mad that some dog owners don't pick up after their precious pooches. With the coast clear, I grabbed hold of Wayne's hand and walked up the concrete path. His firm grip said everything without saying a word.

A distorted image emerged from the frosted glass door panel. On Carla's recommendations, I'd popped into the florist in town and picked up a bouquet of white roses with eucalyptus trimmings before setting off. I'd no idea if Anna even liked roses, let alone flowers. I can't find the words to express how I felt when I saw her. Just a jumble of jigsaw pieces now slotted into place. She was wearing a baseball cap to cover her bald head, but the look in her eyes said it all. While trying not to crush the flowers, I threw my arms around her. It was odd. We both had the same sob. I wonder if our parents had noticed this too.

I held her hand and followed her into a bright front room. There, on a white bulging bookcase, sat an expensive glass jar candle that filled the air with the refreshing scent of lemon and bergamot. Instead of books, an army of Lego figures and creations filled the shelves. Among them were a dinosaur, a boat, and what appeared to be a half-built spaceship, proudly displayed. There was a matching bookcase on the other side of the chimney breast. It contained a collection of children's storybooks and tubs filled with toys. A white coffee table sat between two matching sofas. I picked up a well-thumbed copy of 'And Tango Makes Three'. It's a children's book that tells the story of Roy and Silo, two gay penguins who adopt and hatch an egg. The book teaches us that whilst families come in all shapes and sizes, it's love that glues them together. I couldn't help but notice a menagerie of framed photos of our nephews at different ages sitting on the mantlepiece. It was just a pity that we'd missed out on so much. But at least we were here now. I ran my fingers along the edges of a big white teddy bear throw and tried to relax. Anna played with the zipper on her black tracksuit top, adjusted her waistline, and sat down across from us. Once I'd introduced Wayne, it was time to clear the air. Without giving it much thought, I said,

"I've missed you so much. None of this is our fault, like I said on the phone. I'm sure you don't want to think about all that rubbish right now. All I know is that I love you, and we're here together."

"I couldn't agree more, Max. Life is precious. There's not been a day gone by when I haven't thought about you. Now more than ever, I want my big brother for as long as I've got. Dawn will be back with the boys in an hour when they finish school. I've told them about you both. We always tell them the truth, but in a child-appropriate way. I said that our mother lied and that sometimes adults make bad choices. That's all they need to know for now about that. They've had enough going on in their little heads with me. It's touch and go. I'm doing everything I can to beat this damn thing, but there are no guarantees. I've a double mastectomy lined up too at some point. It's all fun here, not!

"I know things are moving fast, but we're desperate for childcare. It's a real juggling act in between my treatment to keep afloat. Dawn has to work full time to keep the bread coming in. She has two older parents with their own health problems. Whilst they're willing, it's not fair to ask them. And our parents are, well, let's not go there. I've heard that you're a nurse, Max. But you don't need to be a health care worker to see the state I'm in. I'm not much of a mother at the moment. I just haven't got the strength for two boisterous boys, as much as I love them. And it breaks my heart. That's worse than any cancer.

"I've sole custody of the boys. Their biological father turned out to be a complete and utter arsehole. That story can wait for another time though. I met Dawn at work; she's my rock. Let me tell you about the kids before they turn up. Our nine-year-old, Harry, has gone very quiet. Ethan is six and has got very clingy. They're having extra help at school from the pastoral support team. But they're still kids and should have fun.

"With or without the cancer, my boys need to have a relationship with you both. And so do I. I'm ever so grateful that you're here. It's been horrible. All of this has made Dawn and I realise just how alone we are. Depending on how it works out with me, we're planning on coming home in the future and putting down some routes. We can both get transfers to your local police force. I think I've said enough to blow your head, haven't I?"

"No, you haven't. I'm just glad that we can help you. And If you do a Dorothy on us and decide to come home, then we'll be there too. We have some wonderful people in our chosen family. I know they'd throw their arms around you all. It's just like that with them. Wayne and I feel blessed. Aunt Bren would be tickled pink, or maybe purple."

"And that includes me, too. We'll do everything we can to make this work and to help you. Nothing is too much trouble. You'll be sick of us," Wayne said.

For the first time since we entered the house, Anna laughed. She said, "I doubt that. I do. I want to get to know you too, Wayne."

She got up, hugged us both, and disappeared into the toilet. I looked over to Wayne and then the copy of 'Tango Makes Three' again on the table. I slid over to him on the sofa, turned his chin towards me and placed a kiss on those beautiful, full lips. His eyes sparkled back at me. Around twenty minutes later, Anna returned to the room with minty fresh breath and wearing a clean, baggy grey sweatshirt. She propped herself up with pillows and threw a white fleeced blanket over herself.

"Sorry about all of this," she said through her sallow eyes. "I was in the chemo suite this morning."

I'd nursed many patients over the years with cancer, but it is different when it's your own. I looked at her huddled like an Eskimo on this warm afternoon and said, "Don't you worry about a thing."

A rattle at the door changed our lives forever. In traipsed Harry and Ethan, wearing matching V-neck school jumpers, grey trousers and a white shirt with a red and black striped tie. They both had wavy beach blonde hair and matching black-rimmed glasses. An athletic-looking woman with an hourglass figure, short brown hair, and one of the biggest smiles I had ever seen followed them. I looked at the two boys who were hovering with their mum on the other side of the coffee table and said,

"You must be Harry and Ethan. Your Mum has told us what good boys you are. I'm Uncle Max and this is Uncle Wayne. It's very nice to meet you both."

As the two boys squirmed into their mum's blanket, Anna said,

"Go on, say hello. We use our manners in this house, don't we boys? They won't bite you, I promise."

"No, we've had our lunch already. I haven't got room for anything else today. You're both safe."

The boys giggled. The youngest looked over and said, "Hiya, I'm Ethan and this is my big brother, Harry."

Harry half turned from the blanket and said, "Hello Uncle Max and Uncle Wayne."

That was enough. My heart had melted. Once they'd said hello, Dawn asked these Russian dolls to change out of their uniforms. This powerhouse then took me completely by surprise. Instead of the usual handshake, she came over and threw her long arms around the both of us. But somehow it felt right.

"Hiya Boys, it's such a pleasure to finally meet the two of you. Let's just cut to the chase, shall we?" she said, looking at me. "Let me tell you, Anna has missed you so much over the years. It's such a shame that any of that happened."

"Yes, we feel the same way. But Wayne and I will do everything we can to help you both. Whilst we can't change the past, we can certainly change our future."

She belly laughed. "Well, aren't you the regular Maya Angelou? You sound like one of those sodding Hallmark commercials."

And in that moment, we'd clicked. I liked her brand of sarcastic affection. It wasn't long before Wayne and I were sitting with the boys as they read 'Tango' to us. And what an excellent read, made even more poignant because it's based on a true story. Now and again, they looked over at the sofa opposite where their two mums sat. But on the whole, they seemed quite happy to read to us. It just felt so natural and right. Anna's eyes twinkled at me. "You know what boys? This has taken me right back to when your mum was a little girl. When she finished school each day, I read with her too. Isn't that right, Anna? Do you remember?"

She looked over and smiled. "That's right, Max. You are dead good at teaching kids how to read. You see boys, Uncle Max is fantastic fun as well. He's got these daft games that he used to play with me. Do you remember sleeping dragons?"

Before I had the chance to reply, Ethan looked up, jumped in and asked, "What's that, Uncle Max?"

"Maybe one day, I'll show you if you like. Uncle Wayne is brilliant at it too."

Whilst the kids fed their pet rabbit, Anna explained the weekends were tough for the couple. Sometimes Dawn pulled a double shift to make ends meet. The combination of cancer, chemo and childcare didn't mix. They still had bills and with Anna now on half-pay, it was even trickier. We hatched a plan together. Wayne and I intended to come over and play with the boys in their own home whilst Anna was around. If this went well, then she could go to sleep upstairs. Whilst the boys would know that she was still only on the next floor, we'd care for them. Hopefully, this would lead to taking them out to the park in their local area. We planned to increase the time away from the house in order to secure their attachment with us. If all went well, the boys could spend some time in our home and maybe stay over.

My head was buzzing. I was far too preoccupied with our plan than to be bothered by the motorway. All of this time, Anna and Dawn had been within touching distance, and I just didn't know. God certainly moves in mysterious ways. Desperation had drawn us back together, but it was love that sealed the deal. That's the thing about love; it doesn't judge, it doesn't expect or doesn't want. It just silently weaves between us without us even knowing. Oh my God, perhaps I had been reading too many of those cheesy Hallmark slogans after all. Dawn was right! I put my hand on Wayne's hand as he changed gears. Whilst looking at the road in front of him, he said,

"Those boys are something, aren't they? We'll do everything we can to get to know them properly. I know you though, Max, you can't rush this one. Let's just creep and go and see how they respond."

It was scary how well Wayne knew me. I'm sure that he could even tell what I was thinking sometimes. "Yes, you're right. I can be impulsive. But this isn't about me and I can't afford to get this one wrong. And as much as I want to steam in, I know deep down that I can't fix this one. All we can do is to be there and go at the kid's pace."

"Who are you and what have you done with Max? You strange doppelgänger."

"It's a good job that you're driving or I'd make you pay for that, you cheeky sod. Now step on it. I'll show you just how strange I can be when I get you home."

"Promises, promises," he said whilst changing gear, "yes sir, no sir, three bags full, sir!"

# Chapter Twenty-Three

As I went to grab the expensive tea, my fingers got stuck to the greasy table. The smell of sweat and pee completely turned me off. At some point, someone, somewhere, must have waved a tea bag at this swamp. But it was either this lukewarm drink or a slobbery cup of watered down squash to drink. Yum! We'd found ourselves sandwiched in plastic hell. You'd think in my line of work, it'd be water off a duck's back. But without my uniform to hide behind, I was just the same as the rest of the adults. We were all doing our best to avoid a migraine, a dollop of snot, or both. People may've been smiling, but I could tell that they wanted to get out of this screaming hell hole. Wayne wasn't daft. His eyes twinkled as he turned off his hearing aids.

What was Carla trying to tell me, anyway? Before I'd the chance to find out, three dripping bodies appeared from nowhere and wedged themselves between us. They were as warm as toast. Carla laughed and passed the terrible trio a cup of juice. "Well, I never. Just look at the state of you all. It looks like you've been having fun. We've been watching you play. You've been hanging upside down like three little monkeys. Max, did you see them on the slide? They were waving to us?"

Whilst trying to wipe the sweat off these three musketeers with a tissue, I said,

"Yes, I did, Carla. They went down that slide so quickly. I thought Jack Junior was going to lose his trousers when he landed in the ball pit."

Once they'd slurped their drinks, they were off again on a new adventure. Jack Junior lead Harry and Ethan through the maze of tables until they were back in the thick of the soft play area. Over the last few months, they'd developed a lovely friendship. It was great to see them play together. I nudged Wayne, looked at my watch and mouthed to Carla, "Ten more minutes and then we'll go. Are you coming back to ours afterwards? They can play in the garden on the trampoline and the swing together."

She put her thumbs up and shouted over the din, "Perfect".

They wasted no time in dressing up as Iron Man, Hulk, and Captain America. These superheroes were seeing who could jump the highest on the trampoline without falling over. It was lovely to hear them giggle together as we watched them from the piece of the patio. While chomping on a chocolate digestive, I said,

"Jack Junior can stay over if you want a bit of time to yourselves. Christian is off tonight, isn't he? It'll do you both good. We have Ethan and Harry and what's another tater in the pot? Aunt Bren is coming over later anyway. She'd love to see Jack Junior. You know how she is with kids."

I could feel the tips of Carla's soft fingers touch the side of my face. "That's really kind of you. Wayne and you are a natural at this. I can't believe how well those two boys have taken to you both. Forming an attachment is one thing, but supporting them with everything going on at home is an entirely different thing. How's Anna doing?"

Before replying, I quickly swigged down the hot tea. "She's doing really well. Thank god she's come through the chemo and radiotherapy. She's booked in for a double mastectomy. Wayne and I plan to take a couple of days of annual leave so that we can be around during her surgery.

"The community matron team has bent over backwards to support me. Nothing has been too much trouble. I feel blessed. I was stupid to think that they were 'untouchables', as I called them. They're beautiful people. I couldn't believe the response when I went to my new manager and explained the situation too. I have never met such a compassionate and value-based leader in all of my life. Claire really couldn't do enough to help. At one point, I thought she was going to cry with me when I told her about the cancer and the boys. That's exactly what you need, isn't it? "

"Yes, it certainly is Max. It feels like the culture is slowly changing. It's lovely to see that you have settled so well in the team. I've heard that your manager is part of a new breed of leaders who put staff and patients first. I know her of old. She's a respiratory nurse by background, I think. Claire was brilliant with the patients when she was on the wards. There are definitely some good eggs out there now. I hear that the new matron at the Belle Reve is lovely as well."

Wayne raised his eyebrows as he topped up our drinks from the pot. I looked at Carla and replied, "Yes, that new matron is one in a million. A little bird told me she's always going on about her bloody nursing tool bag. She thinks she's Mary sodding Poppins. God knows what the pillock will pull out of it next. I dread to think. It's just a good job the staff think she's *supercalifragilisticexpialidocious.*"

Carla winked and walked over to the trampoline. She said goodbye to the three boys. They were thrilled that they had more time to play together. Before leaving, she threw her arms around Wayne and me and said,

"Thanks boys, you're both brilliant but less of the pillock! If I go now, I have time to have a quick bath and slip into something skimpy before Christian comes home. I've got a little black number that normally gets his engines revving. There's room on that trampoline for another child, after all."

"Too much information Carla, just don't put that image in my head," I said.

Once we fed, bathed, and dressed all three boys in matching superhero pyjamas, we started our evening fun. Even Aunt Bren tried to have a go of the dance challenge. Wayne and I had invested in one of those games consoles where you can create your own avatar. This was purely for the boys of course, and we would never, never in a million years secretly practice in private before they came around. *In the summertime, when the weather is high.* Although it was a tight squeeze, we stood in a row and followed the dance moves on the screen. *You can stretch right up and touch the sky.* The boys were killing it. Their avatars were getting cheers and points flying from all directions. *You got women, you got women on your mind.* However, it's a pity the same couldn't be said for the adults. Coordination and concentration had never been my strong point. I could remember failing terribly during a stint as a student nurse in theatre. No one wanted a scrub nurse who dropped instruments and couldn't remember which one to pass next. I had extra practice, but still couldn't compete with the dancing trio who were bumping elbows together. *Have a drink, have a drive. Go out and see what you can find.* I looked at Aunt Bren, who was doing her best to keep up and said,

"Come on duck, let's leave it to the experts before we slip something, eh?"

"Oh Max, you've read my mind," she replied whilst pulling her necklaces from the back of her perm.

The next morning, a flushed Carla picked up Jack Junior before we got ready to take Harry and Ethan back home. It's amazing how life turns out. Our family tragedy had actually set seeds of happiness. With Wayne firmly behind the wheel and the boys safely strapped into the car, we made our way up the motorway. I really couldn't have given a flying monkey about travelling on it. However, it was probably just as well that Wayne was driving. As we got closer to their home, Ethan said,

"Uncle Max, is Mummy going to die?"

Part of me wanted to lie and reassure him that everything would be fine, but I just couldn't. Instead, I said,

"All I know is that the doctors and nurses are doing everything they can to help Mummy recover. I don't want to lie to you and tell you that everything will be fine, because no one knows for sure. What I know is that both of your mummies love you very much. In fact, we all love you both.

"I think that you're a very brave boy for asking this question. We're all here to talk things through together. Never carry around that big bag of worries on your own. It was lovely to read the story about the boy with the big bag of worries last night before bed, wasn't it? Can you remember some worries didn't feel as heavy once he'd shared them? Now that you have told us about it, how do you feel?"

"The worry is still there, but it doesn't feel as bad now."

"That's a good lad. Thank you for being so honest with me, Ethan. Let's carry the worries together, shall we? Hopefully, they won't be as heavy. And maybe we can just let some of them out of the bag together."

In reality, it'd only been a few seconds but it felt like an eternity before he said,

"Yes, Uncle Max, let's do that. I love you all."

"We love you both, too."

The boys hugged their moms and went to feed Bugs. Once out of earshot, I repeated what Ethan said. We always did this because it was important for us to all to understand the boys' thoughts. Wayne and I had become close to Anna and Dawn. I just wanted them located closer now. Hopefully, the oncologists at the City Infirmary would take over Anna's care after her mastectomy. This grand Victorian Lady had done it again. She was still wrapping her golden thread between us, whether or not we wanted it. What was the point have having a young oncologist in my family if I couldn't pull a few strings every now and again? Well, we had just allowed him to have a night of passion with his wife, after all. It was the very least he could do after that.

---

We'd only gone for a half-hearted look. Never in my wildest dreams could I have imagined that we would be living in a brand new three-bedroom house less than a month after first seeing it. But sometimes in life, things just click into place. After playing cat and mouse for a while with Sally, the sales coordinator, we eventually reached a deal. I thought I was dreaming when she said,

"Yes, we'll part exchange your current house, throw in carpets and flooring and offer you a substantial discount on the new house too. But the deal only stands if you move in by the end of the month. We have end-of-phase one sales figures to meet."

We nearly fell to the floor. But it was real, and it was happening. And that was in the middle of a banking crisis where our monies and deposits mysteriously vanished into the ether before thankfully returning to complete contracts. But a bigger house and garden wasn't about showing off or pretending to be something that we weren't. We simply wanted to have more living space for our family to move around in. Whilst our old home was lovely, and we were very happy there, it was bulging to the rafters with kids' paraphernalia. And although the garden housed a trampoline and swing, that was it. There was no room to run around or kick a ball. I couldn't believe our luck as we opened the door to our new home. From the outside, it looked like how a child would draw a house. It had four perpendicular windows in each corner and a central door. It was this simple symmetry that had first attracted me to this new build. Oh, my god, had I secretly turned into Sister Emily Dickson without even realising it?

"Wayne, I can't believe we can afford this. We're so lucky," I said, looking around the bowling alley of a kitchen diner. "Can you imagine the people we can get in here? The tribe will never want to leave."

"Yes Max, you're right, the more the merrier. I can't wait to get them all over, that is, if I can work out how to use the built-in oven beforehand. We know your culinary skills have got no better over the years, but don't worry. I think we've more than just a couple of plates and a saucepan these days. I won't be serving them an all-day breakfast anyway."

"You'll never let me forget that will you, even if it's true? I'm surprised that you stayed. I was so tired and grumpy after those run-of-night shifts. And you even took it upon yourself to get food and cook for me on our first date. What a man!"

His eyes sparkled, and then he kissed me. "Don't worry, it was the best ten pounds that I've ever spent. You were a cheap date. I knew I wanted to spend the rest of my life making you breakfast, dinner, and tea. And now look at us."

"I couldn't have done any of it without you, babe. I'd probably be lying in a god forsaken hovel somewhere, listening to Blanche Dubois sing in my head," I said. And it was true. Without Wayne, I dread to think where I would've ended up.

That night, we lay on a mattress on the floor of our new bedroom with the rest of our belongings packed in boxes around us. Fresh gloss, new carpet and contentment settled us as we drifted off to sleep. It was nothing short of perfect.

# Chapter Twenty-Four

I had secretly mulled it over for a long time, but was never quite brave enough to do anything about it. These kinds of thoughts take a long time to percolate in the brain before they reach maturity. And once they were out in the open, it would be beyond cruel to change my mind. No one was more pleased and relieved that Anna's treatment had been a success. And whilst the couple were living in the local area now, I didn't want to be just Uncle Max anymore. I also worshipped the ground that Jack Junior jumped upon. He was getting more like his daft uncle every time I saw him. And I certainly recognised the tantrums. Even so, I longed for more. Wayne had always told me I wanted bigger and better. But this was different. It was as if my inner voice was talking to me. And the more I tried to ignore it, the louder it got.

I spotted the ideal place to put my plans into action. The set of draws by the front door in the hallway were perfect. This was the first and last thing to notice when coming in and out of our home. We kept Pongo's old lead in the top drawer, in case we ever wanted to get a puppy in the future. Whilst no amount of words could give justice to the pain of losing him, we were both glad that his suffering was over. His poor back legs just wouldn't carry him anymore. He'd stopped eating and, in the end, just couldn't get up off his bed. It was just so cruel to see him in such a sorry state. He was my best friend, my therapist, and my life. But it was time to say goodbye, no matter how painful it was going to be for us. As the vet prepared him to cross the rainbow bridge, Wayne and I hugged him. Even when it was over, we still cradled him until the vet reminded us we should leave. But how do you say goodbye to someone who has loved you unconditionally for so long? Pongo was our world. But at least now he wasn't suffering. I imagined him making a beeline for Jack and Michael, almost knocking the pair over after peeing up the pearly gates first.

We always dropped our keys off in a bowl on the top of the draws so I knew Wayne would see it straight away when he got in from work. I patiently waited on the sofa and thumbed the corner of a black velvet throw as his key rattled in the front door. He didn't throw his coat and shoes off and find me. But I knew exactly what was distracting him. My heart was racing. Whilst I knew his answer deep down, there was an irrational part of me that worried that I'd got things terribly wrong. He looked so confused as he stumbled into the lounge. He held the soft brown cuddly rabbit towards me and said,

"Max, what's all of this about? Are you serious?"

"I've never been more serious about anything in my entire life. Did you read the note that I left with the bunny?"

"Yes, I did. And that's why I'm confused. You've always been happy being the uncle or godfather. What does this 'Do you want to be a daddy?' card mean?"

The poor man. He was right. But things had changed. "Wayne, please come and sit down with me. I want to talk. I'm not messing you about, I promise. It's just taken me a long time to admit it to myself, let alone you. I want children of our own.

"When the kids went back home to Anna, I'm ashamed to admit that a part of me was so sad. I loved having them with us. I never realised what life was all about until then. And I love Jack Junior so much. But he has his own parents.

"I want to adopt. There, I've said it. We've so much love to give. Maybe we could give a child a forever home. What do you think?"

"Yes, if you're sure, but don't mess me about with this, Max. I couldn't stand it if you changed your mind."

"I know. And that's why I've kept quiet until now. I'm one hundred percent sure we can do this. I've been doing a bit of research in the background. Our local adoption service is putting on an awareness evening soon. Funnily enough, of all places, it's at the Regent Hotel. Shall I book us a place and we can find out more? I love you Wayne. You'll make a fantastic daddy."

The awareness evening couldn't come quickly enough. It was lovely being back at the same venue as our civil partnership. Carrie was standing by the reception desk as we entered. It was like slipping into a comfortable pair of slippers. When she spotted us, she said,

"Welcome back boys, it's so good to see you. I often think about you. I see from my list of registrants that you're here for the adoption evening. It's in the same function room where you had your civil partnership. That's nice, isn't it?"

"Yes, it is Carrie. It's so good to see you too. You all hold a very special place in our hearts."

It was just as nerve-wracking to be standing at the conference room doors. Wayne grabbed my hand as we stared through the crack between them. But this time we weren't waiting for the music to start or a drag queen to interrupt our ceremony. I squeezed his hand a little tighter and said,

"Well, here we are again, babe. I love you just as much now as I did when we were here last time."

He quickly placed a kiss on my cheek. "I love you too, Max. I wouldn't want to be standing here with anyone else."

The doors flung open and it was show time. The adoption team greeted us and made us feel comfortable right away. Matt, a brown-haired, stocky man in his mid-thirties and an experienced adoption social worker, led us to the hot drinks. As we sipped our brew and nibbled on biscuits, he reassured us we were very welcome at the event. No one seemed bothered that we were a same-sex couple. And this was the reassurance that we needed. It was comforting to be back in the same room of our civil partnership. A thousand happy memories bounced around my head. Matt stood at the front of the dance floor where the DJ had set up. In my mind's eye, I saw Adam whisking Aunt Bren around and Danni and Malc line dancing. However, Matt's presentation was equally enthralling, albeit in a totally different way.

He explained that the first steps of the adoption process involved a social worker visiting our home. Adopters come in all shapes and sizes and are all equally welcome. Also, single people can adopt too. During this initial visit, the social worker would glean more general information about our background, health, home and work life. I grabbed hold of Wayne's hand. It was real now and not just a discussion between the pair of us. During this initial meeting, the social worker would discuss the process at great length. We'd then be able to complete a registration of interest form.

We were hanging onto Matt's every word. He said that there are two distinct stages in the adoption process. Stage one is about checks, registration and training. This phase typically takes around two months. We'd need to ensure that we organised stage one with military precision. It would involve us supplying details of people who would provide personal and professional references, going for a medical and attending adoption training. If stage one had gone according to plan, we could move on to the second phase of the adoption process. My heart raced as the social worker explained that stage two is based on assessment and panel. This is the main part of the adoption process, where an allocated adoption social worker would get to know us a little better. During this time, our social worker completes a "prospective adopters" report. This assessment serves as the basis for the adoption panel. Here, our social worker would present our suitability as prospective adopters to a group of experienced professionals. During this formal meeting, the panel members would also question us. The adoption panel considers all information gathered during the assessment process and would make a recommendation on the suitability of us becoming parents. The panel then passes their decision to an Agency Decision Maker, who would have the final say. This decision considers the assessment report and panel recommendations.

If approved as prospective adopters, then our social worker would support us to find a child to become part of our family. This is called the matching process. Wayne squeezed my hand tightly as Matt gave us an overview of this stage in the adoption journey. Matching is key to successful adoption. All social workers involved with the child help in finding the right match. At this stage, our social worker would provide us with detailed information about children in care. This includes their backgrounds and health. If a match is made, we could meet with the child's social worker, foster carer, and family finder. If everyone agreed, then our social worker would present the suitability of this match at a matching panel. Again, the team of experts would interview us during this meeting. The agency decision maker from the child's local authority would ultimately make the final decision on the suitability of a match.

Once the panel matches and approves a child, the adoption team would arrange a plan of introduction. Typically, the team arranges a two-week introduction period, but they can customise it according to the child's specific needs. During this time, the child would move from foster care and into our home. When we had a child living with us, social workers would visit regularly to offer support, help, and guidance. When the time was right, we could then apply for an adoption order after a minimum of ten weeks post full-time placement. Once a family court granted the adoption order, Wayne and I would assume the same rights and responsibilities as if the child were born to us.

My head was buzzing when we left the meeting, armed with far more information than when we went in. The adoption process was rightly thorough and in-depth. The children must always come first. Many of them, through no fault of their own, haven't had the best start to life. Therefore, the adoption process should be robust and rigorous to ensure that each child is at the very centre of finding them a loving forever home. There was no question in my mind that this is what we should do for the rest of our lives. Although we may not change the lives of every child in care, Wayne and I can certainly make a difference in the world of at least one child. Once we were sitting in our car, I looked at the love of my life and said,

"Right then, let's book the initial social worker's visit."

"Are you sure, babe?"

"I have never been more sure of anything in my life. "

# **Acknowledgements**

From the very beginning, when I first started sharing my thoughts and beliefs with the world, I never imagined the overwhelming response I would receive. The support that every reader has shown me has been truly humbling. Each message of encouragement and every word of kindness has fuelled my passion to continue spreading my message of hope and inclusivity. It is because of you, my dear readers, that I have found the strength to push through the challenges and strive to be the best version of myself. I thank you from the bottom of my heart.

It is crucial for those whose voices have been silenced or overlooked to feel validated and heard. Andrew May and the Spectrum Books family have created a safe and inclusive space where all voices are not only welcomed but celebrated. He has paved my path with an abundance of compassion and understanding. For this reason, I will be eternally grateful. Additionally, I would like to extend my heartfelt gratitude to the incredible authors within the Spectrum Books community. Their willingness to share their time, knowledge, and support has been invaluable to me. Being able to connect with such a diverse and talented group of individuals from all corners of the world has been an absolute privilege.

Writing can often be a solitary endeavour, but it is the support and encouragement of fellow writers, reviewers, bloggers, podcasters and all those immersed in this captivating world that truly makes a difference. To all the authors who have shared their wisdom and insights, thank you for inspiring and guiding me on my writing journey. To the reviewers who have taken the time to provide constructive feedback and offer valuable suggestions, I am grateful for your honesty and dedication to help me grow. And to the bloggers who have supported my stories and shared them with their readers, your enthusiasm and support have meant the world to me. So, I extend a massive shout out and sincere thanks to all those who have reached out and shown me the way.

Harvey Virdi, a talented writer and actor, has consistently proven to be a reliable and supportive friend. Despite her busy schedule, she has never hesitated to lend an ear and provide comfort during times of anxiety. Whether I was rambling incoherently or expressing my worries, Harvi patiently listened and pushed me on. I am truly grateful for her friendship.

I'm extremely grateful for the many people and influences who shape my writing. Dolly Parton has provided a constant source of inspiration. Her journey from humble beginnings in rural Tennessee to becoming a beloved country music icon is truly remarkable. Her compassion and kindness have taught me the importance of never giving up on my dreams, no matter the obstacles that may come my way.

If anybody asked me, I would describe myself as a work in progress. To be honest, I don't think I'll ever be 'finished'. But I'm at peace with that too. My new bio-fictional novel, 'That Is What We Are', picks up from where my debut 'How Can We Be Wrong?' ended. I portray my personal and professional experiences of working as a gay nurse in a changing health service. Naturally, I would like to express my gratitude to the many amazing people, both in the past and the present, who have held me up and shown me the way. To protect professional standards and confidentiality, all the patients discussed in my story are completely fictional. However, many patients and their families have taught me so many life lessons over the years. I'd like to express my gratitude to them for shaping me into the nurse I am today.

In my humble opinion, I believe it is love that makes a family. They come in all shapes and sizes and embrace uniqueness. I am incredibly grateful for the support of my husband Wayne, who has stood by my side through thick and thin, loving me unconditionally. His unwavering love has given me the strength to overcome challenges and celebrate the joys of life. And where would I be without my two children? They are the centre of my world. To my children, you are the reason I breathe, the source of my inspiration and motivation. I love you both with all of my heart.

## About the Author

Max Austin has many passions in his life; his husband, his two children, his writing and his work as a nurse. Oh, and not to forget the family dog of course! He lives with his husband, two children and dog in a rather busy but fun-filled household in Staffordshire, United Kingdom. He has worked as an authentic qualified nurse for over thirty years.

Through his writing and lived experiences, Max wants to give a voice to silenced and marginalised LBGTQIA+ groups. He is humbled that his own voice has found a home within Spectrum. Max has been a keynote speaker at LBGTQIA+ inclusion conferences. For Max, kind inclusiveness in health care and indeed our broader society is as vital as breathing.

When not working as a nurse or writing, he loves nothing more than spending time with his children and husband. Most weekends, they can be found covered in mud whilst being led through the park by their rather boisterous but friendly black Labrador!

Excellent LGBTQ+ fiction by unique, wonderful authors.

Thrillers

Mystery

Romance

Young Adult

& More

Join our mailing list here for news, offers and free books!

Visit our website for more Spectrum Books

www.spectrum-books.com

Or find us on Instagram

@spectrumbookpublisher

Printed in Great Britain
by Amazon